Fit-For-Purpose
Leadership #2

LeadershipGigs

WRITING MATTERS PUBLISHING

Fit-For-Purpose Leadership #2

First published in 2017

Writing Matters Publishing (UK)
info@writingmatterspublishing.com
www.writingmatterspublishing.com

ISBN 978-1-9999187-1-2

Editor: Andrew Priestley

Contributors: Jerry Cheshire, Romeo Effs, Baiju Solanki, Sonia Gill, Curtis Harren, David Sammel, Linda Duff, Robert Wilcocks, Kim Newman, Sapna Pieroux, Gaël Reignier, Ian Thomas, Jill Chitty and Andrew Priestley

Dedication

Dedicated to leaders everywhere - and to you -
someone who has decided to step-up
and positively change the world, or *your* world.

Contents

About Leadership Gigs

Leadership Gigs was launched in January 2017 as a global, invitation-only, *WhatsApp* community, for business leaders - CEOs, MDs, executives, business owners and entrepreneurs.

This unique community was created in response to the need of leaders in senior positions for open, authentic conversations with peers. Most leaders don't feel it's appropriate to have that level of self-disclosing openness with work colleagues.

The forum works because it allows them to have totally confidential discussions about problems and challenges with their peers from a broad and diverse range of industries.

The glue, of course, is *Trust*.

Leadership Gigs offers a safe forum for bouncing ideas off one another, sharing, discussing, reflecting and receiving candid, constructive feedback. But importantly it allows them to de-role, share concerns, doubts, express vulnerability and get honest and direct support.

Feedback suggests that being able to talk freely with other business leaders reduces stress and isolation and leads to insights, key light bulb moments and breakthroughs.

The calibre of leaders and the candid exchange in *Leadership Gigs* is practical, insightful, inspiring but above all open and honest.

Are You an Effective Business Leader?

Andrew Priestley

Welcome to *Fit-For-Purpose Leadership #2*.

This book is about self-leadership, leading others and importantly creating an environment and the circumstances for your leadership to flourish.

Leadership is topical and everyone has an opinion on the subject!

On my *Twitter* feed last month there were 397 *Tweets* on leading and leadership - all offering 22 laws, five things, 18 tips, seven principles etc of effective leaders.

I recently *Googled 'How to be an effective leader'* and there is a mind-numbingly ridiculous 405,000,000 articles on leading, so you are not short of advice on how to lead.

Firstly, *Fit-For-Purpose Leadership* is about business leadership - not military, political, or sports leadership - just commercial leadership. So I filtered my search down to *business leadership*.

I read 75 articles for a general snapshot. All the articles give long lists of what to do and how to do it. Much of that advice lacks context and is mostly disorganised and unclear, confusing and contradictory. But it seems they all agreed that effective leaders focus on *performance, developing leadership qualities* and creating a *leadership culture.*

Performance

So let's talk plainly about *performance*. What exactly does that mean; and what bases do leaders need to hit? I am assuming they mean *business performance. Results.*

For context, I will cite UK business statistics. The numbers might differ in your country, but I am confident the ratios will be similar for most developed nations.

- There are 5.5 million businesses in the UK. Three million enterprises (96%) - micro businesses - employ less than nine staff but the average micro business employs 2.4 people.

- 75% of UK businesses have revenues less than £300,000 (the majority earning less than the HMRC £85,000 VAT threshold)

- 20% have revenues between £300,000 and £2 million

- 4% have revenues between £2 and £7 million

- 1% have revenues that exceed £7 million.

- About 0.01% - about 7000 enterprises - have revenues greater than £50 million.

Where does your business sit currently?

- According to the *Office of National Statistics'* 2017 survey of 21 million employees, the average salary is £26,748. If you take out salaries £70,000+ the average wage is about £25,000 and the average junior salary less than £20,000 pa.

- Employment lawyers typically suggest partners need to generate revenues about three times their salary; and you need to generate revenues three to six times to cover junior salaries. Someone on £20,000 ideally needs to be charged out at £60,000 to £120,000 to justify their role. Of course not every business recoups a factor of three - six times salary but that's a general performance target you might aim for if you're self-employed.

What is your wage bill?

I coached a company that employs ten staff with a wage bill around £250,000. Based on a multiple of three that business ideally needs to turn over at least £750,000 to wash its face. It was turning over £475,000. No wonder it was struggling.

(A third of £475k is £158,000. Divided by an average wage of £25k, that business can really only afford 6.32 staff and less with partner salaries.)

As a business coach one of my jobs is to help my clients - no matter what size business - think more strategically about performance - so these are some of the thumbnails I use to generally clarify appropriate performance objectives.

In the above case, we would focus on either reducing their costs, drive revenues to a more acceptable level to justify ten staff; or both.

- You can quickly form a business performance snapshot by dividing your revenues by the number of staff - fee earning or not - to arrive at a ballpark *Revenue Per Person (RPP)* figure.

If your turnover is £300,000 and you employ six people your *RPP* is £50,000. If your business turnover is £300,000 and you employ three people, your *RPP* is av. £100,000 per person.

Ideally once you exceed HMRC's £85,000 VAT threshold you want to aim for £90-100k *RPP.* Performance at this ratio would give you the cash flow to fund sustainable business growth.

I coached a client that employed nine people and their revenues were about £900k - 1million. Nice business.

A basic staple of profitable growth is to sell more, increase prices and reduce costs. And keep your eye on *RPP*. In my experience, businesses that fail to grow routinely struggle with these basic metrics.

The *Office of National Statistics* 2017 survey of 21 million people's incomes concludes that the bigger the company, the more number of employees, and the higher the salary. I would infer, primarily because they have had to figure out how to sustain *revenue per person*.

Here's the point. Whether you are a micro or a corporate sized, *sustainable business performance requires strong leadership.*

A leader who tolerates a poor bottom line, a top heavy team or operational inefficiencies is not leading.

Goals, Purpose and Benefits

From a business performance perspective it often helps to clarify the *goal, the purpose* and the *benefit* of *any* business.

What do you think the *goal* of your business is?

The *goal* of any business is to make money. There is no other goal. That's it. I included the above information to provide a general yardstick on *basic* performance targets.

A lot of people, however, confuse the *goal* with the *purpose*, vision and values, or the *benefits* of the business. Your *purpose* might be to change lives, change the world, solve a problem, true, but the *goal* of every business is to make money.

The *benefit* of making money and delivering on your *purpose* is threefold - 1) the benefits to your customers; 2) the benefits to the business and 3) the benefits to you personally.

To achieve those three outcomes - *goal, purpose* and *benefits* - requires a vision, skill and drive for action. Again: leadership.

Take a moment to consider what does this mean to you?

As a leader - no matter how big your business - you need to know what performance looks like to your business.

I worked with a couple - horticulturists - and the revenues of the business had averaged about £27,400 for over five years. (*RPP* for two employees is £13,700 per person. Ideally, that business should be doing £82,200.)

In this case, we focused on generating revenues. To do that we shifted the focus from *selling plants* to *creating gardens people love*. They still sold plants but upsold gardening supplies, materials, equipment hire, garden design, landscaping services, gardening clinics and even advice.

Subsequently, the average sale went from £27.50 to £375. That business now does about £92,000.

Even if you are a self employed, sole trader your focus is still leadership - if nothing else, self-leadership. If you employ staff then your job really is to lead the business forward.

Regardless of size, your specific leadership job is to:

- Determine strategic direction
- Focus on business performance
- Build a high performing team
- Ensure operational excellence
- Insist on clear business communication

So the question is: that's what's needed but *are you capable of doing that?*

Qualities

Anyone is capable of becoming a leader because leading is a skill that can be developed, but surprisingly few people consider they have the qualities to be a leader.

Most people do not want to assume what they feel might be the onerous responsibilities of leadership. Others lack the ambition to put forward the effort required for a leadership role. *But owner or employee, you are responsible for a result - so that makes you a leader.*

If you operate a commercial venture then your job entails the three key elements mentioned above: you have to state and achieve financial *goals*; you have deliver on the *purpose* of your business; and the business has to deliver *benefits* to everyone that business touches.

That's business leadership. That's what you're supposed to be doing. But what qualities do you need to be an effective business leader?

A quick survey of 75 randomly selected articles generated a list of 43 traits successful leaders supposedly need. This definitely is too big a list for any individual to embrace.

Not surprisingly, most leadership advice books and articles espouse *the* leadership qualities that must be embraced in order to be effective.

Think Colin Powell's 13 traits, lee Iaccoca's nine Cs, the 12 strengths and you get the idea. Napoleon Hill wrote the worlds highest selling personal achievement book *Think and Grow Rich* (1937). He identified 31 leadership skills but failed to reduce that list down to manageable proportions.

A quick factor analysis would cluster separate traits such as *resolve, initiative* and *determination* as one trait i.e., *drive.*

A meta-analysis of the list of traits we sourced reduces leadership down to six key qualities that further reduces down to two long-standing, factors of leadership - *task* and *relations.*

Task is the ability to get things done. Performance again.

Relations is the ability to get along with others and to motivate cooperation, alignment and collaboration. And this suggests creating an environment for effective leadership.

But you and I both know leaders that get a lot done, but kill every relationship; and leaders who have great relationships but achieve little; and we've both certainly worked with leaders who do neither well. Effective business leaders, however, achieve a workable balance between *task* and *relations*.

It might look something like:

Task

- Deciding on a major purpose. This would encompass clarity on vision, values, goals, outcomes etc.

- Developing leadership skills and competencies either through training or experience.

- Developing the drive to achieve the major purpose. This would include attitude, motivation and resilience.

Relations

- Leveraging the skills and drive of others. This would include team alignment and culture.

- Self management. This is obviously personal skills such as traits linked to a professional qualities such as authenticity and integrity; and behaviours such as effective listening and clear communication. Clearly, developing awareness skills would play a major part.

- Management of others would include aspects of management, culture, diversity, and people handling skills.

Achieving that balance between *task* and *relations* leads to the third element: creating a leadership environment that makes that balance possible?

Environment

Our first *LeadershipGigs* book, *Fit-For-Purpose Leadership #1* drew heavily on major trends from corporate wellness. There is a shift occuring from *having to* have workplaces that are health and safety compliant to employees *wanting* to have work for companies that value things like health, wellbeing and wellness.

Our first book focused on key elements currently necessary for creating an environment that fosters that favourable blend of *task/relation* necessary for effective leadership and performance.

Importantly, it focused on three trends: corporate wellbeing and wellness; a growing millennial workforce; and the booming *gig economy*.

We identified six elements that currently appear to underpin inspired leadership environment.

They are:

- **Health** - a growing focus on healthy work places and a new breed of leader that wants to be lean, clean and fit
- **Mindset -** obviously everything on the spectrum from positive affect, attitude, stress mitigation through to mental health issues
- **Social/relational** - the growing need for genuine connection and meaningful relationships
- **Meaning and purpose** - an overwhelming upswing in workers wanting meaning and purpose in their work
- **Best practice** - a desire to ensure that what we are doing in fact leading edge
- **Emerging trends** - coping with changes such as disruptive technology, a fickle millennial workforce or the gig economy.

Fit-For-Purpose Leadership #2 continues this conversation around *performance, qualities* and *environment.* We are proud to showcase another 14 of our *LeadeshipGigs* members - all inspired business leaders - who share their current highest-value thinking around:

- **Health** - Jerry Cheshire (sleep and rest).

- **Mindset** - Romeo Effs (sage advice); and Baiju Solanki (pinpointing strengths).

- **Social and Relationships** - Sonia Gill (difficult conversations), Curtis Harren (conflict), and David Sammel (team communication).

- **Meaning and Purpose** - Linda Duff (finding your why), and Robert Wilcocks (best life).

- **Best Practice** - Kim Newman (collaboration), Sapna Pieroux (your brand), Gaël Reignier (converting) and Ian Thomas (high performing teams).

- **Emerging Trends** - Jill Chitty (social leadership) and Andrew Priestley (profiling).

Once again, it makes compelling reading. Enjoy!

References
- www.researchbriefings.files.parliament.uk/documents
- http://researchbriefings.parliament.uk/ResearchBriefing/Summary/SN06152#fullreport
- www.dailymail.co.uk/femail/
- www.monster.co.uk/career-advice/uk-average-salary

Health

Physical health, fitness, exercise, wellness, wellbeing,
nutrition, diet, exercise, nutrition, sleep,
hydration, hormones, genetics, DNA

Are You a Zombie?

Jerry Cheshire

It's not unusual to hear quotes from historic leaders about how little they felt they needed to sleep, or the importance of sleep with regards to their success. We don't sleep because we want to; we sleep because we *have* to. However, smart sleepers craft their sleep routines around their lifestyle, whilst survivors live their life around their sleep patterns. It's not about sleeping longer, more about sleeping smarter.

Circadian Rhythm

Sleep is an integral part of our Circadian rhythm, often referred to as our 'body clock', which is our physiological connection with a 24 hour day; darkness at night and natural daylight. The word circadian is derived from the Latin words: *circa* for *about*, and *dies* for *day*. During our circadian cycle, our body and mind expect and require regularity of essential behaviours, like eating when hungry, periods of movement, and sleeping when tired.

Sleep – Eat – Move – Eat – Move – Eat - Repeat.

Sleep Cycles

Your Circadian rhythm should not be confused with sleep cycles.

Sleep is divided into two distinct sectors: *Non-Rapid Eye Movement* (NREM) and *Rapid Eye Movement* (REM).

NREM is commonly divided into 3 stages:

Stage N1 is a stage of drowsiness or somnolence. This is the early stage of sleep where we're just about to drop off to sleep. Our muscles start to relax and we begin to lose consciousness of what is around us.

Stage N2 is where we have very little muscular movement and are totally unconscious of what's around us. This stage makes up about 40% of a total night's sleep.

Stage N3 is deep sleep and the stage where night terrors, sleep walking and sleep talking might occur.

REM is the final stage of the cycle and typically makes up about 25% of each night's sleep. It's the stage where memorable dreams occur. This is why, if you remember a dream, you have dreamt it just before you wake up. At the REM stage your muscles are at their most relaxed to the point where they are almost entirely inactive. This incidentally, is why a good mattress and pillow combination is necessary, to support your spine when your muscles do not.

These stages take place about four or five cycles per night and the REM part of our sleep is longer in the two cycles before we awake. A standard pattern would follow this format: N1 - N2 - N3 - N2 – REM

A regular sleep cycle takes about 90 minutes. To sleep efficiently it's important to complete a cycle. If you should awaken before a cycle is complete, your body will identify this and try to adjust itself to compensate. With this in mind, try to sleep in multiples of 90 minutes to maximise the benefits of sleeping blissfully. I refer to this as 'the 90 minute rule'.

Former British Prime Minister, Baroness Margaret Thatcher famously told of being able to survive on as little as four hours sleep per night and claimed: 'Sleep is for wimps'.

It is likely that Baroness Thatcher actually slept for 4 hours 30 minutes each night and this being a multiple of 90 minutes, felt sufficient to her.

A 1/3rd of Your Life

On average we sleep about one third of our lives; about eight hours per night. If you live to be seventy five years old, you will have slept for about 25 years.

Sleep is more than just something we do at the end of each day. It's an essential behaviour, the quality of which will determine our ability to perform daily tasks throughout our waking hours. The better we sleep, the higher our performance levels. Sleeping blissfully also has a direct impact on our health and emotions meaning good sleepers are happier, healthier high performers.

If you divide your 24 hour day into three periods of sleep, work and play, sleep is the recovery from and preparation for work and play. Imagine sleeping for less time, without compromising sleep quality and having more time to either work, or play. This can be achieved by following a sleep routine that incorporates the 90 minute rule.

Polyphasic Sleep

A client of mine was saying that she falls asleep fairly easily when she first goes to bed, but wakes up in the middle of the night and struggles to go back to sleep. My advice to her was to get up and perform some tasks until she felt sleepy again, instead of lying there wondering why she can't fall back to sleep.

A little further investigation found my client was sleeping for about three hours before she woke up (a multiple of 90 minutes). At the end of a sleep cycle, we are almost awake so, waking completely at this stage and not entering the next sleep cycle is something you may easily be conscious of. Later, once she felt tired again, I suggested she return to bed and sleep for another period of 3 or 4.5 hours. This would give her sufficient total sleep over the night, albeit interrupted by a period of activity. This is called polyphasic sleep and is fairly common.

Abraham Lincoln became known for taking long walks around midnight. This suggests he was a polyphasic sleeper and his walks became an integral part of his sleep routine.

'If you can't sleep, then get up and do something instead of lying there worrying. It's the worry that gets you, not the loss of sleep.' - Dale Carnegie

Sleeping Blissfully

Once your sleep routine, including sleeping for complete cycles, is maximised you should expect to experience a multitude of personal benefits only available to those who sleep blissfully. These benefits include a fitter, healthier body, enhanced, happier relationships, and an improved ability to perform tasks and store and retrieve memories. Good sleepers find that they fall ill less, are liked by their friends and family more because they are fun to be around and are more valuable to their business or employer for being more productive.

Healthy Living

Whilst sleeping, our bodies recharge, recover and rebuild vital elements. A stable sleep is the basis of all cures and this is why hospital patients are treated in beds and medical experts recommend sleep and rest to help us recuperate.

People who are sleep deprived are susceptible to falling ill more often than those who sleep well. When we're ill we need more sleep to aid recovery, so by not sleeping well we will take more time to return to full health. During periods of physical illness our circadian cycle is disrupted and our brain becomes confused as to which hormones our bodies require, thus impeding our natural immunisation process.

If you are tired during the day because you haven't slept well at night, you may crave an energy boost from caffeine or sugar based foods. This will unbalance your regular diet and may likely cause weight gain or in extreme circumstances, obesity leading to diabetes.

In a corporate environment, a workforce that remains healthy would mean more man-hours as each member of the team would take fewer sick days. Sleep well to remain healthy; after all, your health is your wealth.

'Each night, when I go to sleep, I die. The next morning, when I wake up, I am reborn.' - Mahatma Ghandi.

Happy Relationships

You know when you have a colleague who is always jolly, happy and smiling? They are full of energy, make themselves busy and are eager to please. You wonder where they get their energy from; right? That's the person who sleeps well.

Daytime tiredness and fatigue causes a reduction in energy levels which can make you feel moody and irritable. At times like this we have less control over our emotions and we may court conflict or become argumentative. This can make us seem grouchy and snappy, meaning we are not fun to be around and this affects our relationships.

We all like to appear attractive and be happy. When tired, you don't look your best. After a good night's sleep you will have fewer facial wrinkles, a clearer complexion, healthier hair, less puffy and brighter eyes. All of this without cosmetics; beauty sleep really is a natural thing.

High Performance

High performers sleep well and poor sleepers perform badly. As you sleep your brain processes information and conserves memories in an easily retrievable order. As you sleep well, your ability to perform tasks, learn and solve problems becomes easier. It's much tougher to learn a task if you're sleep deprived.

Tiredness can lead to memory loss, impulsiveness and poor judgement leading to you becoming more accident prone.

Ex-President Bill Clinton said, "Every important mistake I've made in my life, I've made because I was tired."

Only as you sleep can your body naturally recharge. Your smartphone will lose charge as you use it throughout the day. At night you plug it in to the electricity to recharge. Your body, like your smartphone, needs to recharge and this happens as you sleep. It's important to recharge fully and this can only be achieved by sleeping blissfully every night. Imagine only charging your smartphone to 80% charge, then the following day to 80% of that 80%, eventually the smartphone will just stop working. The same happens to your body if you don't recharge.

Sleep has become an integral part of an elite athletes training regime for preparation and recovery.

Sir David Brailsford of cycling team, *Team Sky* would take motor homes for each cyclist on tour so that the cyclist could sleep on the same mattress each night. Through data monitoring, *Team Sky* knew the correct amount of sleep would enhance a cyclists' performance.

In the corporate environment, sleep can improve employee's performance. In Japan, sleep is tolerated and encouraged in the workplace as a sign that workers are working so hard they've become tired. They call this *inemuri*.

Are You a Zombie?

Using the 90 minutes rule, I have created five categories of sleeper determined by how long you sleep. Which category do you fit into?

As sleeping too long is as bad as not sleeping enough, if you sleep for less than three hours or longer than 10.5 hours then you are a *Zombie* as this is either not long enough or too long to gain benefit from the sleep you take. If you sleep for less than 4 ½ hours, you are a 'sub-somniac'. Here you are gaining some benefit from your sleep, but you could be achieving so much more. Baroness Thatcher may have been a 'sub-somniac'.

Sleeping for 4.5, or 6 hours puts you in the *Survivor* category. This is the category into which most people fall. Most feel comfortable with this amount of sleep, but may be unaware that sleeping longer would almost certainly make them feel so much better.

When you sleep for 7.5 or 9 hours, you are a *Super-sleeper*. This is where the magic happens and people who regularly sleep for this long really feel a plethora of personal benefits experienced only by sleeping blissfully.

Sleeping for more than 9 hours but less than 10 ½ makes you an *Over-sleeper*. The extra sleep is a waste of your time. Beyond 10 ½ you're a 'Zombie' again.

The Routine

As we lead our busy lives, keeping to a routine for anything becomes a challenge. However, having a sleep routine can help you lead a happier, healthier, more productive lifestyle and unlike an exercise regime or diet, can be easily implemented. After all, you're going to sleep each night, just try to be better at it. Usually, we know what time we need to wake up as we set an alarm to wake us. Work backwards from your wake up time in multiples of 90 minutes. If you wake up at 7.30am, go to bed at 10.30pm or midnight. This will give you optimum sleeping time of complete sleep cycles.

Once this routine becomes habit, add a *leading up to bedtime* routine and a *first thing in the morning* routine. Together, you should find yourself sleeping blissfully and reaping the rewards.

Sleep tight.

Jerry Cheshire is the proprietor of leading independent bed and mattress retailer *Surrey Beds*, recently awarded *Independent Retailer of the Year* by *The National Bed Federation*.

As creator of *The Beducator* character Jerry helps consumers cut through the marketing hype to have the knowledge to buy the correct bed and mattress.

He followed this with *The Beducator's Blissful S.L.E.E.P Method* to ensure each buyer sleeps well in their newly acquired bed.

Jerry has extensive knowledge of the UK bed and mattress industry, having been active in this market since 1997. He has established relationships with most of the largest manufacturers and many of the industry's leading protagonists.

As a supplier of his own range of *Reedham's* brand pillows, he has relationships with leading UK bed and mattress retailers and is familiar with legislation and safety standards to which furniture and bedding products must comply.

Jerry is an active public speaker promoting the benefits of *Sleeping Blissfully*. His first book *Sleeping Blissfully – How To Make The Most of A Third of Your Life* is available from November 2017.

www.beducator.co.uk

Facebook/thebeducator

Twitter/thebeducator

www.surreybeds.co.uk

jerry@surreybeds.co.uk

Mindset

Psychology, motivation, development, experience, upbringing, self-talk, emotions, feelings, resilience, emotional intelligence, self-worth, perceived ability to control, mental health

Leadership Lessons from my Grandmother

Romeo Effs

Growing up in Jamaica with my Grandmother, she always told us as children to have *manners*. She always said to us, in her thick Jamaican accent – *"Manners will tek yuh roun' di world, suh mek sure you have it".* Translation – Good manners will take you through and around the world so make sure you develop and display them at all times.

As a kid, I often thought she was referring to my table manners or to saying good morning to persons as I pass them in the streets – yes that was customary and woe be unto you if someone older told her that you passed and didn't greet them. As I grew older however, I came to realise that what she was referring to was *character.*

You see, my Granny was a poor simple woman. The only material riches she had was the two-bedroom, predominately wooden house in a rural village in Jamaica and a *Singer* foot pedal sewing machine, which she used to earn a living to help take care of the eight grandchildren and two adopted children.

Looking back, I can now see that she had far more wealth than material riches. She lived a pristine life. One that was spiritual, God fearing, doing good for others and living a life of the utmost integrity. She had high ethical and moral values, which was reinforced by her daily reading – bible or other inspirational material. She spent her time listening and advising people and talking about community concerns, and what they

31

could do to help others who were less fortunate in the village. I never heard my grandmother speak badly of anyone, and she built very strong relationships with those around her.

She also had this amazing ability of reinventing herself. Always developing new traits and habits to adapt to any situation life would throw at or place her in. She constantly maintained, developed and grew her manners ... her character. She was an inspiration to me and many others and a true leader.

So, what does this story about my grandmother have to do with leadership, you may ask? It's about the element that is the foundation of effective leadership - character. In order for you to be an effective leader and achieve long-term, positive impact on the people and organisation you lead, you need character. Great effective leadership starts from the inside, because ultimately what's on the inside manifests and finds its way to the outside. You can plaster yourself with all kind of social persona and labels – the aspirational view of yourself, but you will be found out eventually as your true self will be revealed sooner than later. What we all need to understand is that leadership is an inside out job and the quicker you realise this, the better.

It is important therefore to work on developing you, nurturing and adding fuel to the fire within, in order to emit to those, you lead your true authentic self. Among many other things, there are four keys pillars that I have learnt from my grandmother that helped me to build a sound character and hence be the leader that I have become today.

Traits/Habits/Mannerism

This is the foundation of what shapes your character as a person and even more so as a leader. Good traits take time to develop into good habits, and your habits are what you are judged by as a leader. These habits are also the models that those you lead will emulate, practise and follow.

I was involved in politics from an early age. I worked as a Political Strategist and Researcher for Prime Ministers, Senators and Members of Parliament. At one point, the Leader of the party I was affiliated with, was viewed as autocratic and dismissive of anyone who opposed him. Those were traits that eventually became his habits.

Those who were closest and loyal to him – his tribe, developed the same habits, and treated people in the same manner resulting in internal anarchy. As a leader, you need to consistently nurture your good habits so that they will eventually supersede any negative habits you might have or develop.

Keep growing and adding fuel to your fire

Character is the foundation of effective leadership, and it is in a constant state of flux. You have to work at it to keep it in tact and to be consistently better at it. If you don't, it will slide. As they say *garbage in, garbage out.*

Character building has to be something we give attention to daily. We are human and left to our own devices, we are going to fall from grace. So, watch what you read, listen to and observe.

I was once in a relationship and for the last three years of that relationship we lived together.

During that time, I didn't grow and develop as a person and neither did my character. I was constantly surrounded by negative energy and influences - the movies we watched, the stuff we read and listened to. I thought, by engaging and participating in these activities I was ensuring the survival of the relationship. In fact, it did the opposite, as resentment, anger and frustration set in for both of us until the relationship eventually ended bitterly.

My lack of growth was evident to those in my team and clients as they realised that my spark had disappeared. I had to take corrective action.

I started reading again, listening podcast attending conferences and events that stimulated my mind, help me to grow, build and added fuel to the fire.

Iron Sharpens Iron

It is often said that you are the average of the 5-10 people you spend the most time with. I saw this clearly growing up as a child. My grandmother insisted that we should not speak to, play with, or keep company with certain other kids in the village. She would get really upset, even to the point of us getting a real ass-whooping, if she found out that we disobeyed these instructions.

Those who you surround yourself with, will either influence you up, laterally, or down. Like an aircraft, you don't need baggage that will weigh you down, you need thrust that will help you to lift off and take flight.

I have a simple philosophy – if I am the brightest person in the room, I look to change rooms. As a leader, you must also want to surround yourself with people who you can learn from. You develop and grow as a leader when those around you are moving in the same upward direction, and who you can get answers from to be better.

You have to make an effort and be far more intentional about the people you surround and spend time with. If you want to be a great effective leader, then spend time with those who you consider great effective leaders.

Build strong lasting relationships

My Gran had a saying: *True friends are better than pocket money.* I have experienced this in a number of ways throughout my life. As a leader, you need to building a strong reinforced inner circle of person who are not afraid to call a spade a spade and to tell you as it is. This is vital to building your character.

What I have found is that having an inner circle of close

persons that you can bounce ideas pass, or talk to openly and freely, and who are also not afraid to be candid and transparent with you, helps to keep you balanced and in check. It helps you to rationalise if you are making the right decisions at times and if you are on the right track. Sometime by just having someone to reason things out and get honest feedback, helps you to come up with the answers related to integrity, morality and ethics that plaques all leaders.

THE EQ Grandmother

My Grandmother was a true leader. She was the matriarch of the family, a leader in her church, and she had tremendous influence in and over the affairs of the community we lived. Looking back, I think my Gran probably discovered *Emotional Intelligence* (EQ), as she was the first leader I saw displaying and using the traits of the now famous technique, long before 1990 when it became a corporate jargon first used by Daniel Goleman.

Although Goleman stumbled across the term in an academic journal, his bestseller, *Emotional Intelligence: Why It Can Matter More Than IQ*, was responsible for the EQ's foray into pop culture. The components of EQ vary but Goleman six traits closely resemble the leadership traits I grew up seeing my Grandmother display:

- **Emotional Awareness:** You understand the emotions you are feeling and how those emotions affect your behaviour and your performance.

- **Accurate Self-Assessment:** You are aware of your own strengths and weaknesses, and are open to feedback and learning from your experiences.

- **Political Awareness:** You are aware of important formal and informal relationships that exists and the dynamics at play as a result. You know who are friends with whom, and how things actually get done.

- **Influence:** You are skilled at gaining consensus and drumming up support for your vision, your projects, and the things you want to achieve. You challenge the status quo and enlist the support of others.

- **Communication:** You can read between the lines when conversing with others, speak in a straightforward manner and seek mutual understanding and feedback.

- **Conflict Management:** You address problematic situations proactively, with tact and diplomacy. You encourage open discussion and help to orchestrate mutually beneficial solutions.

A lot of these qualities go hand in hand. Leaders who have strong political awareness are often good at internal persuasion and conflict management. Who my siblings and I have become is a direct result of the leadership influence, values and beliefs instilled in us by our Grandmother.

Now that I am a leader in my own right, I use these lessons of character building and emotional intelligence to empower others and to ensure those I employ in my businesses, perform at their highest and best versions of themselves. I am constantly building on the other foundations of my leadership to make it stable and to keep my character in check. Here are just some of the things I practice to help me achieve this:

- **Practice generosity and compassion.**
  I love developing people, that is why I do what I do as a High Performance Executive Coach and Business Mentor. When I work with my clients I get them to a heighten stage of awareness where they are able to listen carefully to input and recognise the emotions that direct the behaviour of others. In this way, both they and I get more out of every relationship and interaction, whether business or social.

- **Make *being yourself* safe.**

  I show my team that it's more important to be completely authentic, to engage in all aspects of the business and to always deliver on commitments, rather than to be admired and adored. I encourage them to cultivate genuine self-awareness so they accept mistakes, flaws or failures, and to be open to receiving *constructive* feedback.

- **Leave time for play.**

  A big part of what I preach and teach is *enjoying the process*. It's also part of our company values – *Have fun at every stage*. I encourage and practice spontaneous jokes and safe pranks within the team, because imaginative play is vital for social and cognitive health.

  It decreases stress and renders us more emotionally *in tune*. Physical activity in particular has a positive effect on the brain and helps people expand their emotional horizons. Hence, I encourage my clients and team to do some form of physical activity. I am super active – I meditate daily, do Yoga at least one per week and do an intense gym workout 5 - 6 days per week.

- **Create your own legacy**

  I mentor my teams on how to manage sticky situations and overcome obstacles. I engage them in frank conversations on the political nuances in the organisation to eliminate guesswork. I facilitate self-reviews of performance, asking employees, *how do you think you did?* or *what do you think you could have done better?*, to hone awareness of individual strengths and areas for development. One of the things I am known and respected for is managing critical and reputational damaging business crises for our clients. Instead of handling these crises by myself, I allow my team to engage and participate fully in the action and learn how to influence and resolve these issues.

What I have come to believe is that the secret to lasting impact, long-term success and leaving a dent in the world, is to really focus on development your personal character. That is what is going to carry you through as a leader when you are faced with the difficult choices, when you hit setbacks or have to deal with challenges, which is inevitable in your journey as a leader, whether in your business, the corporate environment or your personal life.

All I can say is, thank you Granny – Iris Bruff (1920-2008).

Romeo Effs is Founder & CEO of *Empire Builders*. He is an award-winning serial entrepreneur, and is one of the UK's top *Coach and Problem Solver for BAME Corporate Leaders and Entrepreneurs*. He is an Author, Speaker, Hollywood Producer and former C-Suite Executive who have worked globally with top *Fortune 500* companies at the senior executive/board level.

Romeo became a Senior Executive at the age of 25, and has never worked below the Senior Executive/Board level since then.

He started his first business at age of 16 and has owned and operated an incredible 20+ businesses becoming a millionaire before the age of 30. One of his companies became one of the largest event management company's in the Caribbean allowing him to work with A-List celebrities such, Luther Vandross, Mary J Blige, R. Kelly, Cedric The Entertainer, Kymani Marley, Steve Harvey, Sean Paul, Kenny G, Arturro Tapping and Gladys Knight just to name a few.

Romeo is an expert in helping *BAME* senior professionals and entrepreneurs solve problems, manage crisis, build dynamic reputation and make quantum leaps in their life, career or business. He brings an amazing experience with over 25 years' as a boardroom level corporate executive and serial entrepreneur.

Game Changing Multi-Dimensional Leadership

Baiju Solanki

This may sound obvious, but you do not need a title to be a leader. Leadership is an attitude; it is a mindset; a behaviour that can be seen in many forms.

Leadership is multi-dimensional. You can think of one leader in one situation being very different to another leader in another situation. For instance if we attempt to list all the qualities that make a good leader (as many have) what each one has in common and then look at what makes them different, the list can become blurred.

One person's way of being assertive and taking control of a situation is another persons dictatorship. That is why context is so important when we look at leadership and especially game changing leadership.

The future of work and the impact of rapid socio-economic change requires us to adapt quickly and embrace multi-dimensional factors of leadership. The leaders of the future will not fit one mould. Complex and often challenging scenarios increasingly demand different types of leadership working together to manage change.

How might we approach multi-dimensional leadership?

A body of research conducted by Dr John Mervyn Smith, looked at the kind of talent needed for the ever changing future of work and business.

His initial research looked at the a group of leaders referred to as *Game Changers* and what made them different. His team found that like entrepreneurs, *Game Changers* have an appetite for risk: they see things in the world that others do not see and they are obsessive about making their ideas a reality.

Particularly interesting in the research was the discovery that there are in fact four leadership roles that are required for a team to deliver the outcomes and impact described in a variety of contexts.

Smith's team used the research as the basis for the development of *The Entrepreneur Impact Profile* powered by *The GC Index*, a framework for empowering entrepreneurs and business owners to maximise self-awareness and leadership to make an impact on the world. *The Entrepreneur Impact Profile (EIP)* describes five profiles of leadership:

The Game Changer sees *Possibilities*

The Strategist sees *Patterns*

The Implementer sees *Practicalities*

The Polisher sees *Potential*

The Play Maker sees *People*

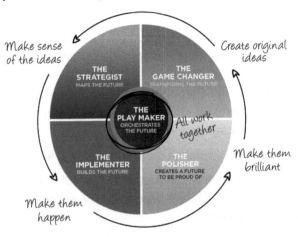

Each leadership role in the framework is described below:

The Game Changer

- Game Changers see possibilities.

- They see ways of doing things that others do not. They have a way to imagine how things could be and when they become obsessed with an idea, how things should be.

- Their potential contribution to an organisation is radical, rather than incremental change.

The Strategist

- Strategists see patterns and brings excitement and energy to tasks.

- They will enthuse and influence others with new, creative and innovative approaches to doing things.

- They tend to be more interested in the ideal rather than the real: genuine satisfaction comes more from generating the idea rather than realising it.

- They will have the business acumen and analytical skills to convert ideas into commercially focused strategies.

The Implementer

- Implementers sees practicalities, and 'get things done'. They just deliver.

- Their philosophy and practice is one of practical and pragmatic problem solving.

- They will often have a reputation as a 'safe pair of hands', someone who can be relied upon to get things done in a dependable way.

- They are outcome focused and will get things done without being a 'slave to the process'

The Polisher

- Polishers see potential and symbolise the philosophy and practice of 'continuous improvement'

- They seek to set the standard for excellence within their role and organisation.

- They can adopt products, processes and procedures with patience for incremental change, and constantly seek to improve them.

- At their best they will be able to understand and articulate the commercial, competitive advantage derived from continuous improvement.

The Playmaker

- Playmakers see people and invest in their relationships with people.

- Their focus is on getting things done through the strength of their relationships and through shared endeavours and teamwork.

- They enable rather than delegate and take pleasure in seeing others 'shine'. They like to get the very best from others.

Traditionally leadership was examined from the perspective of personality – the qualities of an individual way of being rather than doing. The *EIP* enables a new perspective on leadership that is multidimensional, focused on strengths and works with how an individual's natural ability to make a contribution in the world.

The profile itself aims to identify and score your natural leadership preference and style, and provides another view of how we might develop and support leadership in teams and businesses.

Leadership is now longer about a title but, how you *show up* in the world and play to your strengths. Leadership is no longer just about personality, but is concerned with what you do and the many different dimensions required of leadership roles. Using the combinations of the five profiles we have identified 10 multi-dimensional leadership roles.

The Comtemporary Leader –sees the patterns and trends in their world. They can predict the ways in which events will unfold. They can articulate this change is a way that engages others; they 'take people on the journey' that means that they can shape events rather than just react to them. They are at the leading edge of change.

The Visionary Leader – sees the patterns and trends in their world. They can predict the ways in which events will unfold. But they see the need for changing these traditional and historical patterns, for doing something radically different to change the ways in which people live and interact.

The Traditional Leader wins by getting things done; they can be relied upon to deliver. They are seen to have the talent to lead an organisation at a senior level if they can also put delivery - operational goals - into the bigger, strategic context.

The Charismatic Leader sees a different world, but a new world that can only be realised through the endeavours of others. They have the charisma to engage others with their vision and to orchestrate collective endeavour.

The Inventor leads with an obsessive focus upon turning a transformational idea into a tangible reality. They lead with the example of persistence and resilience and a strong belief in what is possible. They will inspire people in this regard

The Creative Problem Solver will live by the mantra: "I can see a better way of doing this" and they will see things that others do not see. They will lead by inspiring hope that there is a way through a problem / obstacle that had defeated people up to that point.

The Leader As Coach helps people to see what is possible and to realise that potential. They know when to be directive and 'hands on' and they know when to stand back and let people shine. They lead through their commitment to and belief in others.

The Inspirational Leader, challenges individuals and teams to be the best that they can be; to aspire to perfection. They have an ideal in their heads and engage others in realising that ideal; ultimately to achieve their dreams.

The Driver brings the right mix of pragmatism and perfectionism to getting things done. Their relentless focus upon learning and continuous improvement will fuel others. This is with an optimism about what is possible, as well as giving them a sense that they control their own destiny.

The Aspirational Leader leads with their predictions about the future. These will be based upon the patterns and trends that they see in the past. They will bring an academic rigour to their thinking; their concepts will be coherent and their arguments sound.

CONTEMPORARY LEADER

Angela Merkel *(Strategist/Playmaker)*

VISIONARY LEADER

Elon Musk *(Strategist/Game Changer)*

TRADITIONAL LEADER

Ana Patricia Botin *(Strategist/Implementer)*

CHARISMATIC LEADER

Richard Branson *(Game Changer/Playmaker)*

INVENTOR

Coco Chanel *(Game Changer/Polisher)*

CREATIVE PROBLEM SOLVER

Henry Ford *(Game Changer/Implementer)*

LEADER AS COACH

Ghandi *(Playmaker/Implementer)*

INSPIRATIONAL LEADER

Anita Roddick *(Playmaker/Polisher)*

DRIVER

Martin Luther King *(Implementer/Polisher)*

ASPIRATIONAL LEADER

Evita Peron *(Strategist/Polisher)*

Figure 2. GCI Multi-Dimensional Leadership

If you look at some of the leadership combinations of famous leaders above you start to see how leadership is made up of different strengths.

Let us bring this closer to home, and imagine a small team led by an entrepreneur who fits the *Strategist/Game Changer* profile - *The Visionary Leader.* As a game changer, new thinking and challenging the status quo will drive the team.

Her leadership style would energise others and help them see a new future. Combined with the *Strategist* profile, she begins to see can how to map out a plan and prepare for implementation. But as her combination of leadership skills will mean that implementation will remain elusive.

To back her up and deliver game changing impact, this entrepreneur would need a *Traditional Leader – Strategist/ Implementer,* and *The Driver Implementer/The Polisher.*

When you look at the *Traditional Leader*, they have a natural proclivity for analytics, mapping out the problem and also making things happen by implementing strategy. The combination of different traits, both for the *Visionary,* and the *Traditional Leader* and the *Driver/Implementer* is priceless. Together, these strengths create game-changing possibilities.

With a multi-dimensional model of leadership new insights into game changing teams becomes possible. Leaders themselves can begin identify whether they have the right leaders doing the most impactful leadership roles in an part of the business.

Teams built on solid leadership qualities will always thrive. Understanding what steps lead towards establishing a game changing team is critical. We know that the key to success is to transform individual action into collective power. With the right team each member becomes capable of making a game changing contribution. These are the four critical steps:

1. DEVELOP STRONG VALUES

Spend time developing a set of strong values to demonstrate what we stand for.

Employees and often customers will buy into our vision, share our values and help us develop and turn great ideas into reality. The right leader in the right team will make this happen.

2. FOCUS ON IMPACT

We can all make a positive impact. You can make an impact on:

- Yourself
- People around you
- The world

Now is the time to focus on the real impact that we personally can make and others within our team by focusing on who is *best* for the job at hand.

By understanding how each person will make an impact and what each person can contribute to the team, or the project or to the wider organisation, we are far more likely to create a game-changing culture that in turn surfaces individual leadership qualities.

3. IDENTIFY GAME-CHANGING TALENT

Identifying and embracing *Game Changers* is critical to long-term business performance.

It is important to help *Game Changers* understand the contribution other people make, and how others can help realise their game-changing idea. Using the *Entrepreneur Impact Profile* will help understand their talents.

4. FOCUS ON CULTURE

In today's fast-paced digital world it is important for everyone within the business to feel they have the freedom to challenge things. We need everyone to be looking for new opportunities.

We also need to get everyone to start shifting their mindsets and put contribution and impact at the heart of everything they do. This focus on contribution will ensure we all make our game-changing contribution.

New models of business, need new modes of leadership. With the *EIP,* it now is possible to ensure that the right leadership, combined with mutually supportive talent can foster business growth, culture, individual talent, and above all strengthen teams to meet the challenges of a rapidly evolving economy.

Award-winning business man, author and *TEDx* speaker *Baiju Solanki* is now the CEO/ Founder of *EnSpirit Global*: a platform that serves to awaken, instill and enhance the entrepreneurial spirit in all of those who wish to live their best life.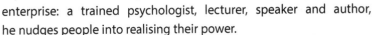

As a former businessman of the year, his experience extends beyond the realm of enterprise: a trained psychologist, lecturer, speaker and author, he nudges people into realising their power.

Baiju has experience in the academic world, as a psychology lecturer, and in the corporate world as a sales director, before starting his own coaching & training business in 2007.

Using his skills as a trainer, teacher and coach, he aims to transform the world through teaching entrepreneurial skills to business people, those with start-ups, students and employees – all to increase productivity, performance and winning mindsets.

His mission is to teach people that being an entrepreneur doesn't really have anything to do with business: it's a mindset centred on making the most of what is available to you in life now, and thriving. He seeks to unleash the entrepreneurial mindset in others.

Baiju is the author of *I'm An Entrepreneur - Get Me Out of Here* available on Amazon.

www.EnSpirit.Global

www.baijusolanki.com

@baijusolanki

We Need To Talk

Sonia Gill

Words we know to mean it's time for a serious chat. A difficult chat. One where we'll say or hear something we might not like. And as leaders it is something we must do and must become skilled at.

In the first half of this chapter I'm going to look at why successful difficult conversations are so important and in the second half I'm going to share how you can avoid the most common mistake made in difficult conversations.

Part I: Why are successful difficult conversations so important?

Conflict is the currency of leadership

As leaders a core part of our role is to have difficult conversations with people: about their performance, behaviour or attitude. I've not met anyone who likes conflict, I've met a few people who appreciate its importance, but mostly I meet those who know they need to get better at it. As leaders we don't have a choice about managing conflict, it's an inherent part of our role. Yet sadly most people aren't trained on how to create healthy conflict.

Why do I have to manage conflict?

I know it would be nicer to avoid those difficult conversations, they're not fun at all and trust me I don't like them either. And you can avoid them as long as you're prepared to accept that your team will not be as good as they can be and high performance will be a long way off. Also, whilst some issues will resolve themselves or go away, many will get worse and fester until it reaches a breaking point and you will have to deal with it. It's far better to tackle the issues early and iron out those wrinkles before they become stubborn creases!

You might be aware of the research by Bruce Tuckman (Tuckman, 1965) on group formation. He noticed that groups go through four phases:

- **They form** – come together, get to know one another and understand the aims of the team.
- **They storm** – they test the boundaries, vie for position and test one another.
- **They norm** – they establish their code for working.
- **They perform** – they focus on their shared goals and how they can work together to deliver them.

Tuckman noticed the importance of storming, that teams who learnt to storm well (have conflict and difficult conversations) were able to perform better.

Think about it. You've got a difficult member in the team, you tread eggshells around them and they make meetings, decisions and the atmosphere awkward. Yet they do their job well enough and are in work every day on time. Is this working as well as it could? What if they didn't create an atmosphere? What if an honest dialogue could be had with them? How would that improve the team's performance and happiness?

In my work creating higher performing teams I see this and many other examples often. Issues like this drain energy and time away from the job you want to be doing.

The cost of conflict

A powerful way to bring this to life is to look at how much conflict is costing you. Here's a simple sum to work it out.

Estimate how many hours per week are spent on conflict in your team or organisation. This should include:

- Difficult conversations.
- Conflict.
- Accountability conversations.
- Gossip.
- Talking about staff performance or conduct.
- Performance improvement meetings (not your planned annual performance meetings).

Take that number and complete this sum:

_____ X48* weeks   =_____ X £25 p/hour**

                          =_____ Hours per week

Annual time

Annual cost

* A 52-week year less 4 weeks holiday.

**Make this an average hourly rate for your team/ organisation. At the time of writing the average UK hourly salary is £13 per hour

Figure 1: The cost of conflict

Amend the numbers to reflect your organisation.

This is the most basic and tangible cost of conflict, how much time and money is being wasted on conflict in your organisation? As a result what opportunities are being missed because your team's precious time is being hampered by conflict? And what is the stress of conflict doing to their productivity and well-being?

Tackling conflict well can reduce all of these negative factors dramatically and it has the greater benefit of making your team higher performing.

So what have you got to lose from becoming good at conflict?

Why is it so hard?

I want you to tackle conflict situations. That might be someone who is frequently late, someone who is snippy with others, someone who you feel is lazy or someone who doesn't support the team. Whatever uncomfortable issues there are I want you to tackle them well.

But I understand that it is hard. Conflict is a psychological 'fight or flight' situation and by asking you to wade in and talk about the issues that need to be talked about I'm asking you to go into something that will trigger the fight or flight instinct. This is an older, more basic part of the brain at work and it's why you don't like conflict.

Learning some skills and techniques can help you have these conversations more effectively and reduce the fight or flight instinct, opening the door to having a more successful difficult conversations and resolving the conflict issue.

What is the definition of a 'successful difficult conversation'?

Quite simply it is a difficult conversation that creates positive change, quickly and kindly.

This contrasts with the definition of a 'difficult conversation' which is a dialogue about a situation where something needs to improve and voicing the issues is likely to upset someone to some degree. (If you're sure someone won't be upset then it's unlikely to be a difficult conversation).

Part II: The most common mistake made in difficult conversations and how to avoid it

The hardest part

Getting the conversation started is not only hard but it's the piece of the puzzle that is most likely to go wrong. I've been training people on how to have successful difficult conversations for over six years and this is the most common mistake I see people make.

By not starting the conversation for success you can find the person doesn't hear what you're asking them (even though you think you've been clear), the conversation gets pulled off track and the change you want to see doesn't happen. If that's what happens you're better off not having the conversation at all because it won't move the situation forward.

But, get the start right and you will be on the path to success. It's not the only aspect of having successful difficult conversations but it's certainly one you can put in place quickly and see it make a dramatic difference.

The only part you can script

The start of your conversation is the only part you can script. There's not much point in planning the rest of the conversation because it rarely goes the way you think it will. And if you start the conversation well you'll find that it often goes better than you thought it would.

Getting the party started

My structure for starting the conversation, which has worked successfully in all of the hundreds of conversations I have supported, is this:

I, issue, the outcome

The commas demarcate the three sections.

1. Start with 'I'

I is less accusatory then *you* and it helps depersonalise the conversation. You might say: I feel, notice, believe, observe, think – whatever words are right for you.

2. The issue

Now clearly and specifically state what the issue is. Avoid broad, abstract words, the more concrete and specific you can be, the better.

3. The outcome

Now say what you would like to happen. This is not to *talk about the issue* as I've seen many people say, that's a method; it's the end result you want to achieve.

This is actually quite a hard sentence to construct, but the payback for getting it right is huge: the issue will move forward and often you won't need another conversation. How often do you find you brave a difficult conversation only for it to not go well, the change not happen and you need to find the energy to talk about it again? We want to avoid that and this sentence will help you.

Let's look at some ways you can make sure your opening gambit is excellent.

Tip 1: The mistake within the mistake

I've seen people put the *I* and *issue* firmly in place but the bit that is forgotten, more often than not, is the *outcome*. This is actually the most important part of the sentence. If you only said the outcome you would start the conversation well. In not having a clearly stated outcome you don't anchor the conversation and you don't give it direction.

The outcome is usually the opposite of the issue:

- Someone is being late – you want them to be on time.

- Someone is not doing the work to the required standard – you want them to do the work to the required standard which means it needs to x, y and z (you would be specific about the work and what moves it up to standard).

- Someone challenges ideas aggressively – you would like them to challenge ideas constructively.

The outcome can seem blindingly obvious when you state the issue, but say it anyway. This is to reduce the likelihood of you needing to have another conversation, if you can fix the issue in one conversation that's better for all. A clear outcome will make this more likely.

Tip 2: Have examples

There are lots of nuances to successful difficult conversations and no black or white rules save for one:

If you don't have examples to back up the issue you are raising, you don't have the conversation.

Whatever issue you raise you must have concrete examples that you can share with the person:

- If they were late – when? What dates and times? The more specific the better.

- If they're not doing the work to standard – what work? When was it done? And what specifically is sub-standard?

- If someone is aggressively challenging – when did they do it? What did they do? What was the impact?

You will use these examples if the person doesn't agree with you ('I've not been late') or to they help the person understand why you are saying what you are saying ('I'm not aggressive, I'm robust'). If they are aware of the issue then you don't need to use the examples. It's best to have a bullet point list of three so you've got them should you need them.

Tip 3: The solution siren

When working out your sentence there is a secret siren calling you into the rocks with their enchanting song. She wants you to put the solution in the place of the outcome: I notice you've been late on three occasions over that last two weeks and so I need you to leave home earlier.

The underlined section is a possible solution, I say possible because it might not work. The real outcome is actually: I notice you've been late on three occasions over that last two weeks and I need you be ready for work at 8:30am every day.

Can you see the difference? The problem with the first one is that might solve the problem but it might not. In stating the outcome the person knows what you want and they are best placed to know what will fix the problem. You might need a discussion around that, there might things you can do to support, or it might be something they can do once they have clarity of the outcome.

Tip 4: Write it out

This is the only part of a difficult conversation you can script, it might take you 5-10 minutes but it's well worth the investment in time. When you're working out your opening sentence write it out. Then improve it. Then improve it again. Then improve it yet again. You should have written it out five times, improving it each time. You want a clear, crisp sentence, that isn't too long. To help you with this I have one more tip.

Tip 5: Watch out for 'fuzzy' words

These are words like *better* or *improve*, words which can be misinterpreted so you need to be specific about what you mean by *better*. I once had a leader say she wanted a member of her team to *lead better*. This was way too fuzzy. In fact what she wanted was for higher quality planning and three specific elements around that. *Lead better* could have been wildly misinterpreted, so be specific and concrete in what you're asking for.

"The experience of being understood, versus interpreted, is so compelling you can charge admission"

Joseph Pine, author of "The Experience Economy" (Pine, 1999)

There are many elements to making a difficult conversation successful; getting the conversation started well is one of the biggest.

Please don't underestimate how often you start a conversation badly, I say this because I see it all the time – and every time that person thinks they have been clear. If someone walks out not having heard the message you wanted them to hear well, I hate to say it, but it's because you didn't deliver the message.

Apply what I have shared with you in this chapter and you will see the success of your difficult conversations increase. Good luck!

References

- Pine, J. H. (1999). *The Experience Economy*. Boston: Harvard Business School Press.

- Tuckman, B. (1965). *'Developmental sequence in small groups'.* Psychological Bulletin, 63, 384-399.

Sonia Gill, Author, Founder and Director of *Heads Up*, is an educational leadership coach who supports school leaders create *Outstanding* schools.

As a qualified teacher, she has taught every age from reception to Y11, and is also a successful business leader, leading multi-million-pound businesses and teams of hundreds.

Since founding *Heads Up,* she has personally supported hundreds of Heads and school leaders create a culture of excellence.

Sonia found that there is a qualitative difference in taking a school to *Good* and leading a school to *Outstanding* – being outstanding is all about creating the right culture. She takes schools on the journey to excellence putting in place three core leadership strategies.

At the time of writing all of the schools Sonia has worked with, and have been inspected, have improved by an average of at least one Ofsted grade.

Sonia is the author of the #1 ranked book *Journey to Outstanding* and *Successful Difficult Conversations* released January 2018.

Contact

Sonia answers a question on having successful difficult conversations every week. You can ask her a question at:

www.ukheadsup.com/ask-sonia

www.ukheadsup.com

info@ukheadsup.com

@SoniaG_HeadsUp

Social

Quality of life, quality of experience, quality of environment, connection to family, friends, community, work, social, relationships, stress

Having Courageous Conversations

Curtis Harren

What do you think having Courageous Conversations means?

What does it mean to you? What comes to mind? Is there a sense of fear or vulnerability or a sense of "better to bottle things up and move on"? In many life and business situations, we are often afraid to express our sincere thoughts and feelings because we are unsure of the outcome.

For years I didn't speak up at meetings, speak out at behaviours that I didn't think were acceptable nor did I have the courage to express my innermost emotions for fear of judgement, of being labeled, not measuring up, of not being liked, fear of not being heard ... does any of this sound familiar? This happened at work and at home until I was eventually slammed in the face with a series of healthy doses of reality: a lost job, a big investment loss coinciding with a business closure and a near loss of my marriage!

It wasn't all bad, I experienced a smattering of successes, but there was a recurring pattern of fear.

When my gut told me to speak up, my "what if..." fears stopped me.

When my heart told me to speak out, my "OMG, what if..." fears rendered me speechless.

When my head told me to share my ideas and concerns, my "who am I to…" fears and "worthiness" emotions overtook my actions.

Hopefully sharing some examples from my life will help you to draw from your own experiences and maybe we can all change our communication patterns and improve our successes.

At my lowest point, my business was failing, I was struggling to be positive, to rise up and succeed despite many creative approaches. Turns out, it was quite possibly my best year yet, despite the horrible things I was going through. It forced me to look at myself and my life in ways I have never been able to, or even thought of before! It was the kick I needed to change my life.

Looking back at my failing business and my crumbling marriage there was one common thread. I wasn't facing the very root of my issues; disconnect with my emotions and therefore not being fully present with the most important people in my life and work.

My biggest lesson was the freedom that came from having the courage to speak up and have uncomfortable or difficult conversations. Talking to my business associates about what I felt had been going wrong. Talking to my wife to learn why she wanted to leave. I learned this from having the courage to speak and openly listen to others. By opening up to my wife, she found the courage to express her concerns in return and we were eventually able to heal our relationship. I suddenly heard her in a way I never heard her before! By speaking up at work about a situation I will explore later in this chapter I was able to be proud of myself like I have never felt before.

I share these examples because having a *Courageous Conversation* is not just about talking, or listening, it's more than that. A *Courageous Conversation* is not a casual talk; it's one that faces emotional elements.

In business, decision makers will often have different

opinions. Everybody has their own ideas of how to run a company and what is the *right* plan of action in various situations. Speaking up and not having fear to express what is important and right for you is the first step! Your opinions can significantly change the course of action in your life and your business now and in the future. Speaking up and being your authentic self will mean there are no regrets.

A *Courageous Conversation* <u>must</u> have three key elements:

- **Empathy** (the conversation is not just about you)
- **Being Present** (Fully engaged and fearless of the emotions at play)
- **Committed to being authentic and trustworthy**

Ideally both individuals will bring these elements to the conversation. But realistically, one person will be driving the conversation and the other will be faced with dealing with reactionary emotions. It takes courage from both individuals; one to face the potential *wrath* or *hurt* of the other person by broaching the subject, and for the recipient to bravely listen and feel the driver's words without being defensive and to truly empathising with them and how they've been impacted.

As you read this, my greatest hope is that you relate your own stories to my writing, for you to be in touch with your own emotions, as well as others, around events in your life to see the truth for yourself. Perhaps you're feeling over-whelmed just reading this. Good! Being present in your own emotions as they emerge is critical. Is there fear or anxiety? This is normal, we all fear unknown consequences. But now think of the consequences of *not* speaking up or *not* taking action.

Which risk is truly greater?

Before we continue, let's consider a few scenarios where having a *Courageous Conversation* might have changed an out-come for you, or for others.

Over the last 20 years, the explosive adoption of email and other forms of digital media in Businesses and other organisations has had dramatic effects on how we communicate. It has resulted in far too many superficial or dismissive conversations and avoiding difficult conversations. *When was the last time you felt terror when faced with having a conversation with someone? Did you have it?*

I liken the emotional outcome of an avoided conversation to a dagger. If you have ever had an emotional experience, or was ever the recipient of one of *those talks* that seem to come *from nowhere*, you might relate to the feeling of a dagger to the gut.

Conversely, this also happens to those who build up enough courage to finally speak up. Often there is so much fear about the kind of reaction they will have to endure it can take weeks, even years, to get their words past their lips. So a *Courageous Conversation* absolutely has to include how the conversation is received.

We are always responsible for our behaviours and how we communicate through them. This is especially true for those entrained behaviours *that just happen* during our conversations. Being aware of your behaviour, particularly in the moment is the first step, making a conscious decision to change is the second step and consistently making the effort and putting in the work to change is the third step. It's an ever evolving circle. In addition to these 3 key elements of a Courageous Conversation, the following behaviours are also required.

Being Present

To be *present* in your *Courageous Conversation* is absolutely critical. It is particularly important on the receiving end, regardless whether someone has approached you with the courage to face you or whether you have faced them and they have then turned back on you.

To explore this further, consider this drawing:

Tracking	Active Listening	Being Present
Only listening to answer, sell or put in the time. Often happens when multitasking or not paying attention.	Analytically listening to understand intention and meaning. Considered effective listening.	Similar to Active Listening but without the mental activity. All senses and emotions are involved. Highest order.

In each of these three frames we see three common types of listening; arguably the most important part of any conversation. Listening can make or break the outcome of any conversation. I remember once starting a difficult conversation with one of my boss' to address his unacceptable behaviour in one moment - I was brought on board to create stability and effective communication in the organisation so staff could focus on doing their job.

This one incident undid an entire year of effort in trust building and cultural change. The behaviour was unacceptable and counteractive to all of our efforts to build up a productive and high performance team environment.

So I addressed it!

What I encountered was the *first level of listening* as I tried to impart on him what he had just done to the organisation (and *undid* what he really wanted to accomplish with his team!).

I had to face the full brunt of his fury the entire time, until he finally got into the active listening stage so we could actually deal with the end goal. Reflecting back on that day, I was *fully present* through this whole experience. I never raised my voice, I never let my anxiousness get a hold of me, I knew what had to be done and why. I remained cool and calm and it was infectious.

So what was the outcome of this *Courageous Conversation*? Before the day ended he made a public apology to the entire team for his tirade.

Being present isn't about being emotionless, it's much more about being fully aware and in touch with *all* the emotions going on inside and being OK with it. Feeling each and every emotion. By being more present, all of my relationships have deepened, I have experienced less anxiety, I have more clarity of how to behave better and all of my communication has become more effective.

Observing others, I've discovered most people are fearful of having *Courageous Conversations* because they intuitively know the other party is unlikely to be in a state of active listening let alone present listening.

As you witnessed in my story, by starting a conversation while in a state of being present, and remaining calm, you will help to get the conversation steered in the right direction.

Regardless of the other person, you will have expressed your thoughts, unloaded any burdens you were carrying inside, and most importantly you will have no regrets because you were honest and authentic. Start small, with friends or family and see how your life can improve today!

Being N.I.C.E.

One of the keys that I learned as a people pleaser, was that I often held back from having a *Courageous Conversation* because I was afraid to hurt others feelings, or to be seen as not being nice. But I've learned it's actually more cruel to not speak up. Perhaps they will put themselves in jeopardy if something isn't being said. Perhaps you will save their business a lot of grief, customer dissatisfaction or lost revenue by speaking up. *(What are those compared to a little fear of speaking up and may be hurting someone's feelings in that moment? Which do you think they would appreciate more? Which would you appreciate more?)* I realised I needed to be N.I.C.E. to be a better friend or co-worker. What I mean by this is that I say to myself **"No!** (Don't be afraid), *I Care Enough"* to speak up and let them know, even though it's quite uncomfortable. This also applies to yourself, you need to care enough about yourself that you will speak up so you don't have a lingering "I wish I said something..." nagging you for the rest of your life.

Let go of FEAR

At the start of this chapter I wrote a lot about fears and how they intertwine in our lives and hold us back. Remember:

FEAR is your choice:

Forget Everything And Run, or

Forgive Everyone And Rise.

In order to have a *Courageous Conversation* we need to let go of our fears so we aren't even faced with this choice. This way fear doesn't even have a grip on us. But easier said than done! Right?! In times when I've faced my fear, one of the biggest was being afraid to admit I even had fear, I felt held back like elastic bands adding resistance as I tried to move forward until they snap back. I've since learned that it's far simpler to just turn around and lean back into them, in other words, lean into my fear and accept it, this releases the tension of those *elastics* and when the tension is low enough I can just uncouple them from me and release their hold on me. Then I can walk away.

The story I shared earlier about facing my boss' wrath I had to face all this emotional tension and more. The fears I needed to release were plentiful; job loss, income loss, loss of the people around me, judgement by my wife for losing my job, fear of not being able to provide for my family, to name a few.

But there was also the fear of guilt for not standing up for the right thing, for not having the courage to speak up, to be seen as weak *in my own eyes*. By leaning into all these fears I was able to clearly see what to do. Ultimately it was easy to speak up and to challenge a man who easily held power over others simply because the benefits outweighed my fears. The benefits were more than I could ever have predicted, especially in confidence and pride in myself.

So, by now you should have a good idea about why we should have more *Courageous Conversation*, but how do we initiate one?

- Be Present in your thoughts and emotions
- Consciously choose to be *N.I.C.E.*
- Let go of fear, and know it's the right thing to do!

Whether at home or at work, and no matter what kind of relationship you are facing a *Courageous Conversation* in (customer relationship, co-worker, child, friend/foe, boss, spouse, loved one, etc) the backbone of all healthy relationships is forthright, honest and respectful communication.

The core of this is trust, and at the core of trust is doing the right thing. It's about doing the *tough* things such as sitting with your feelings.

Spend some time each day thinking about your impulses and mindless habitual behaviours and ways in which you can improve your self-control and self-discipline.

Having *Courageous Conversations* is just as important as having quiet time in building a healthy life for yourself. Practice everyday, try to stretch it out, be fearless in being yourself and speaking out. Having a say in everything you do, or don't do is the core strength from which we are capable of giving and receiving real love and support.

Author's note

While I have discussed the importance of being fearless of emotions, whether of others or of your own, I am assuming you are dealing with people of sound mind.

I must qualify this that if you feel *unsafe physically* around a certain person or situation, then please take appropriate actions to protect yourself. Unfortunately some abusive situations cannot be solved by conversation alone.

Curtis Harren, MSc, MBA is an experienced business coach, entrepreneur and founder of *CEOcopilot* and is building the *Unconditional Man* movement.

He specialises in helping professionals and their teams increase business performance by improving communication and simplifying their systems.

In addition to working with individuals and teams he also provides corporate employee leadership development programmes.

+1 (403) 804 9972

curtis@CEOcopilot.com

www.CEOcopilot.com

www.Facebook.com/CEOcopilot

www.twitter.com/CEOcopilot

www.linkedin.com/in/curtisharren

Building Trust in Teams

David Sammel

True trust between teammates is rare. Superficial trust is common. The depth of understanding and communication that precipitates an unbreakable bond is underestimated. A high level of empathy and maturity is needed to accept each team member as a whole – warts and all.

It is a decision to believe and know that everyone in the team has the same objective and intent, that everything that anyone does, is done for the good of the team. This means that any mistake is instantly forgiven and the rest of the team will do their utmost to help rectify or mitigate the error.

There is an understanding that attempting to achieve anything significant will come with challenges and often the risks that must be taken in meeting these challenges by default will lead to mistakes.

The quest for a team that intrinsically acts as one is built on experiences that bind people together and take time. This journey is one of levels, a journey that cannot exist without a clear intention to reach the goal of deep trust. The perseverance to become open and honest about feelings and doubts so that these can be addressed and totally understood is how the process grows. It is both a painful and glorious journey to explore ways to build a team's psychological strength through forensic examination of the self and how that affects others, so that performance becomes an orchestra of each person's strengths complementing weaknesses and when it fails there is support and acceptance without a hint of blame, only a determination to improve and 'go again'.

I'm going to highlight a live example of a doubles team in tennis on a quest to become the best in the world whose journey is not yet complete, but is a wonderful example of how difficult the stages of development are as they climb the levels of teamwork.

This is a case study of a recorded conversation from a time when the team was at a low point and trust was being severely tested after a string of losses.

David Sammel (DS): I'm going to lead, because I think there are some things that need to be heard, which I started in New Zealand and Australia where I said – *"if you're going to be really good, you have to be incredibly honest and in doing so, you will feel vulnerable."*

In life everything is perception, and most people just take the perceptions and run with them. But if you're going to be a top doubles team, you've got to know what each other's perceptions are. That means opening your mind to each other, with your inner thoughts. When people say *there's no hiding place*, very few people know what no hiding place means. It means you are literally sharing what's in your head, and it is a skill that needs learning.

That often means hearing things that are difficult, but if you don't get to that point then you will never have the honesty needed for sustained growth and success.

You might ask how there are some teams out there that do extremely well, who maybe haven't been through this? Well, my theory is that a lot of great results are achieved through momentum, and self-responsibility.

When two players that are very self-responsible, get together and get momentum, they can do some amazing things as a team and when they run out of steam they usually split. Then there are the special teams that stay together, like the Bryan brothers. I would say that the Bryans are probably the greatest ever because they are twins. They intrinsically knew what each other's thoughts were, and then they were brave enough to go there over and over again, until they just operated very openly with each other. That made for an amazing team.

It's very unusual for a team to go through a process to where they truthfully open up to each other. You guys are fairly honest, but have some way to go.

Your relationship is great *off* the court and great *on* the court most of the time. But there are some cracks under pressure, and that's what we've got to eliminate.

Individual connection is great, but today I saw, and occasionally have seen it before, where you go into your silos. *You're each in your own minds.*

Although you're talking about the points, there's no real connection anymore. You're each stuck in your own stuff. Remember, at that point, that's when some perceptions deep inside start to play out in your minds about each other. That's what we have to explore.

Leadership. This is the big question and I'm going to go through my perception of what's happened, and why you're not yet a team of leaders.

Basically, if you're going to be the best, you've got to find a way for two alpha males to co-exist as leaders. It's inherently unstable. You've got two alpha males who are both leaders. You wouldn't be ranked as high as you are if you hadn't been able to lead. This is not unique to you as a team. All teams have this problem, because if you're going to be successful, you have to survive in a sport full of alpha males.

How do these unstable situations survive?

Basically, one becomes the leader, either by acceptance or by consent, or what often happens, is in each person's own mind, they *both* believe they're the leader, but then never actually verbalise it.

They are either successful for a while, or when they are not, they split. Therefore, so few good doubles teams stay together through the tough times.

In tough times, if in your mind you believe you're the leader, you can easily think you're the better player. So why would you stay with anybody who is not pulling their weight?

This is the problem most go through. But I believe that you are mature enough, and want success enough to go through this process to understand how leadership is going to work. Two highly driven, alpha males *can* lead, but *both* must come to the table with an openness, even if that means pushing through initial discomfort, to find the optimal operating mind-set.

Don't forget, we're talking about high-level tennis as well as anyone who operates at the elite level. It may not involve obvious or huge shifts in mindset. Often success is more about subtle shifts in the mind.

Y, you said something to me today that I think really opened this up for me. You said when X served at 4-1 in the breaker, and had a misthrow, that made you nervous, *because you thought he was getting nervous.*

Player Y (Y): But it's not an excuse. It was my fault, I know, I missed this easy volley. I put wrong words in my mind at that moment.

DS: Yes, but that is because I think you're starting to feel a responsibility, that under pressure, you have to come through, because he might not. That's why the wrong words enter your mind; and that needs to change.

I'll say this: *all blame and excuses start as good reasons.* Good reasons are a more sophisticated way of having an excuse.

This is why I say, inside your head there's a slightly deeper thought which is, "I was nervous, because I felt his nerves and by default I missed because of him", yeah?

Y: Mm-hmm, yes.

DS: But at 4-1, you guys were dominating but your perception was *X* got nervous. That perception caused you to tighten up. That can't happen. But it's real because it happened to you. This is where the trust in each other becomes real. In that moment, you have to trust that *X* will do his job, *whether he has a misthrow or not.*

Nobody is perfect, so screw-ups will happen. What I saw today, which was disappointing, was due to the underlying stuff inside your heads. Once *Y* had mucked up, there was no real fight because you were each in your own space. Neither of you grabbed a hold of the other one to say, *"F*ck this, we're connected. We have to go again."*

It can happen where one goes into himself, but, when both of you go into yourselves, then the talk between you is just BS, because *you're both not there.* The goal of conversations like these is to help you become more aware so you have a better chance to snap out of it. You fight to the very end, no matter what screw-ups have happened. There is so little wrong with the level of your tennis. There's a little more wrong with how you guys are leading and taking responsibility on the court.

Player X (X): Today at 4-1, I wasn't nervous on the serve. I think I caught the ball maybe three times in the match, and this was one of those times, but it wasn't anything special. It's the negative way you reacted to the situation that bothered me.

Y: Yeah. I know it was my fault, I apologise.

X: But this is what we're talking about now. It's like the stuff underneath that makes you have this reaction, because it comes from somewhere.

DS: I don't think your reaction to Y missing the volley, was strong enough either in terms of support. We know in a *breaker* if you miss a *sitter*, it hurts. The person who hasn't missed must step up in that situation and go, "No biggie, it happens. Let's go again!" I'm not sure the second mistake would have happened had there been positive interaction to the first miss. *Y* needed your leadership and a show of confidence, after the miss.

Today this is what it came down to: *what were you about?* There was nothing left from 6-5. You weren't about anything. The other team could *feel* this and immediately relaxed and you guys were just muted. You did not push back.

That's because there's underlying stuff going on that needs to be swept away. I said to Y earlier today it's like having a very clean room and you've got to go in with a searchlight and find the little teeny bits of dust and get rid of them.

Once you've gotten rid of that dust, it's not like second-guessing, "Did we get rid of that dust, or not?"

No, get rid of that dust and it's gone. Look, you guys are good together. We're sitting here well inside top 25 in the world this year. However, I don't think either of you, yet, get how *strong* you must be to win a *Slam*.

What underlines where you are at this point is a need to step up and get rid of any doubts about each other. When you doubt each other you are basically doubting the team and you can't do that anymore. Nerves is one thing; doubt is another.

"I'm tight and I need help, give me more", or "I'm tight but I'm going to step up". That's how you speak about nervousness. We all know that you won't come through every time, but it's about winning more often. Knowing that this is how you will deal with tension, you can get rid of the BS that if you feel the other guy is nervous, that tightens you up. You feel him tight, you read the situation and say "Come on, I trust you, you can do this."

Then get on with your job.

You're both good enough tennis players to do magical stuff in this game. Yes, you have to work at this, because don't think that this is it ... the awareness and understanding is only the first step.

The second step is becoming better and better at implementation. The third step is where your trust is so high you rarely need to implement, because you just are.

When you just are, is when you win something huge.

I want to emphasis that this is not just about tennis. If you think this is about tennis you've missed the point. This is about self-leadership, leading, leading under pressure and what can and does go through the minds of high achievers in leadership roles.

David Sammel is an in-demand consultant in leadership, sought after speaker, the author of *Locker Room Power* and the coach of pro tennis players.

He is an expert at finding the small margins to help already successful individuals and teams across a spectrum of sports - and leaders in any industry - find another level.

https://www.lockerroompower.com

https://twitter.com/DaveSammel

Meaning and Purpose

Spiritual, values, ethics, moral behaviours, legacy, generativity, rehearsing the future

How to Find Your Why

Linda Duff

When a business leader finds their Why and takes action, amazing things happen. But for many, discovering that fundamental purpose seems a mysterious process. *Start with Why* says Simon Sinek. 'But how?' many people reply, 'And how will I recognise it?'

In this chapter are two tools:

- A method to find your *Why;* and
- How you can know for sure that you have found it.

Ray's Story

Ray Anderson was a successful man. Approaching retirement, he was reflecting on the future of Interface, his $1bn commercial carpet business as he watched his grandchildren play. He had been tasked with making an announcement on his company's sustainability policy - and there wasn't one.

Suddenly he was struck by the oddest sensation. It was as if a spear had pierced his chest. In that moment he realised that his industrial practices made him one of those responsible for jeopardising the future existence of the planet for his beloved grandchildren and their children, even though his production plants were legally compliant.

This epiphany transformed his purpose and mission: he committed to finding environmentally sustainable ways to make carpet, then a heavily oil-based industry, that left a zero footprint on the earth yet were productive and profitable. He called it *Project Zero*.

Ray set about modelling his plants' processes on the cycles of nature – recycling and repurposing, using only inputs that created environmentally neutral outputs, easily absorbed by nature. As Ray said, if he succeeded in such an oil- and pollutant—heavy industry, anyone can do it.

Between 1994 and 2008 he revolutionised his factories. The results? A 78 per cent reduction in CO_2 emissions; removal of toxic smoke stacks and water pollution; productivity doubled and profitability tripled. He attracted extraordinary talent, enthused by *Project Zero*, to develop the new systems and technology. Employee engagement at all levels was second to none and, most importantly, customers sang the praises of the products and service.

Ray died in 2011 but his mission continues: his factories will be totally environmentally neutral by 2020.

Ray's big *Why*, his deeper purpose, began with his love for his grandchildren and the recognition that his business practices were impacting on the continued existence of life on the planet for their future. He realised the truth of this through a power-ful physical and emotional pain response that felt like a spear through his chest. His response to finding his purpose has been literally world changing.

Why We Need a How-To

I believe that we need a method to get clarity on our *Why* because it can change: through life circumstances, a crystalising event, or in the natural process of personal evolution to the next stage of life.

Ray was approaching retirement and saw he had two potential legacies to leave: that of a successful industrialist who would be proved by history to be an environmental criminal; or a courageous pioneer who contributed to saving the planet for his grandchildren and future generations.

A real-life Superhero.

The tool that follows can be used when you've lost sight of what feels meaningful to you. When life has become dull, repetitive and you know you are capable of so much more, when you feel off track and dissatisfied. At times like this would it be useful to have a method to help you re-connect with the deep driver that gives your life true meaning, your purpose?

The Route

In his *Golden Circle*, Simon Sinek shows that your *Why* is not found in the rational, logical thinking mind but in the limbic system that governs emotions.

So, if your purpose can't be figured out with the rational mind, how exactly do you reach it? The answer: to access the limbic brain, we must go through the emotions. The route to the emotions is through the body. For many, this is a road less travelled. We'll walk that road shortly.

How do you know when you have found your purpose?

Ray's epiphany was accompanied by a powerful physical experience, like a spear through his chest. This was how he knew that a profound truth had come into his conscious awareness. He felt it with his body accompanied by a knowing, not just as an idea in his mind.

On uncovering their purpose people often feel a strong emotional response along with tears – not tears of sadness though. The tears come from feeling that something inside has finally lined up. It feels like a relief. You have accessed a deep truth about yourself which may have been long-forgotten, denied or buried in a life of 'getting through' and compromising on your dreams and visions. Like when you're moved by something of great beauty, a piece of music or an expansive view in nature, you know it in your heart.

The body's strong physical sensations may include: an electrical impulse moving through the spine; expansiveness in the chest area; a sense of energy rising or sinking in the gut; a change in body temperature.

To realise your purpose is a key moment, a revelation. You feel and know it from your body and from your emotional response. As the limbic system is not directly connected to the speech centre, you may not be able to express it in words straight away, which is why you need to allow yourself plenty of time.

A method to connect with your body and emotions

Sit comfortably, upright in a chair and take some time to scan your body checking that it is relaxed… the muscles of the face, shoulders, arms, torso, abdomen, legs.

Take five long, deep breaths. Close your eyes. Take some time to tune in to the inside of your body. What do you notice?

Find the strongest area of pain, tension or pleasant physical sensation. Focus on that area and spend a few moments observing what you notice. What emotions are you aware of? What feelings are there? Just observe. Repeat this for two more areas of the body that want your attention.

Notice what's there.

A Method to Discover Your Purpose

While connected to your body and emotions, try this method to discover your purpose.

It involves repeatedly asking a question. Each time you ask the question, it takes you to deeper level until you get to the root cause or foundational reason, your purpose.

When mining the earth to get to the precious diamonds or gold, you drill down through the layers of soil and rock. The precious gems and nuggets are not found on the surface. It's the same with your purpose. It's not found in the normal, everyday state of the thinking mind. If it were, you would have found it long ago.

Here is a first question with variations, choose what works for you:

'What is your purpose, what do you want to achieve, what is your deepest vision for yourself/your business?
What do you REALLY want?'

Stay open and curious to what comes up, maybe words, an image or a sense of knowing something. Trust the first thing that you notice.

You can tell it's coming from the right place if it's: expansive, life-enhancing, simple, is for your good and you recognise it as true. Stay open and neutral to what arises.

Anything judgemental, negative, doubting or fearful is coming from elsewhere. Ignore it and ask again.

Then ask:

'If there were a deeper purpose beyond that, what is it?'

Breathe, take your time, check that you are connected to inside your body. Again, notice what shows up.

Say 'Thank you'.

Keep asking this same question and stay open with your body, to what comes. Keep going through the layers, patiently asking and waiting for the response.

As described above, when you get to your purpose your body and emotional response will tell you. Take time with this. Then it's time to celebrate!

An example with Dean

First Question: What is your purpose, what do you want to achieve, what is your deepest vision for yourself/your business? What do you REALLY want? Give lots of time to answer.

Answer: To make £3 m profit in my business.

Question: 'If there were a deeper purpose beyond making £3m profit, what is it?' (Give time.)

Answer: I want to make a lot of income as the business owner.

Question: 'If there were a deeper purpose beyond making a lot of income as a business owner, what is it?' (Give time.)

Answer: I want to be financially secure.

Question: 'If there were a deeper purpose beyond being financially secure, what is it?' (Give time.)

Answer: I want to live in a good neighbourhood.

Question: 'If there were a deeper purpose beyond living in a good neighbourhood, what is it?' (Give time.)

Answer: I want my kids to go to good schools.

Question: 'If there were a deeper purpose beyond wanting your kids to go to good schools, what is it?' (Give time.)

Answer: When I was growing up I lived in a bad neighbourhood and went to a bad school that didn't teach me what I needed to get ahead and be successful. I came out thinking I was dumb and it took me years to realise I was actually okay.

I DO NOT WANT THAT FOR MY KIDS! I want them to go to good schools so that they learn, do well and don't waste their lives like I did.

How did Dean know he'd connected to his underlying meaning and purpose? A palpable, strong emotional charge came with the words above in capitals. He felt a *grabbing feeling* in his chest accompanied by tears that welled up in his eyes. Dean's Why is to give his children the best opportunities in life.

You can use this method by yourself: record the questions, connect with your body and emotions then play the questions, pausing the recording between levels for as long as you need to – that way you can focus on staying with your body and staying open to what comes up.

Or you can get someone you trust to read you the questions. Let them know beforehand to give you plenty of time for the answer to come, ensure they fully accept and respect your responses and that it's not appropriate for them to add their own opinions!

Get a Coach

If you are new to working through the body this way, I recommend that you do the process with a coach experienced in this method.

The first time you do anything new or different you are forging a new neurological pathway in the brain. The logical mind finds all sorts of reasons not to do it. 'It doesn't work', 'I don't get it/ can't do it' etc. A trained professional knows how to move you through if you get stuck, and to keep going until you get there.

Take a First Step

Once you know your purpose, straight away take a first step to set it in motion, make a phone call, schedule a meeting, do some research. Use the momentum you've created to begin your journey along the new path immediately, however small the step.

As a business leader, knowing your deeper purpose is the key to successful outcomes for your business, customers and staff. Your purpose flows into every area of your life: family, health, community and life balance. I believe that your purpose changes as you go through life. When you've lost sight of your purpose, you feel dissatisfied, restless, and you know you aren't doing your best work. With this powerful method through the body and emotions, you can find your purpose. You can be sure that it's real from your emotional and physical response.

My wish is that you keep discovering your purpose, take action and create your legacy that makes a real difference, like Ray did.

References

- Sinek, S. (2009) *Start with Why*, Portfolio Penguin

- Anderson, R. (2009) *Confessions of a Radical Industrialist*, RH Business Books

After working in scientific research, **Linda Duff** moved to a corporate career in IT before leaving the UK to start a property investment business and raise her three daughters in rural New Zealand.

After triumphing over depression using holistic methods, Linda became passionate about our innate abilities and human potential.

Since 2004 she has had a private practice as a *Journey Practitioner*, working one to one with business leaders and corporate clients helping them resolve past trauma and clear blocks to their success resulting in extraordinary turn-arounds.

After completing the *Visionary Leadership* programme with Kevin Billett in 2011, she is now focussed on leaving the world in a fit state for future generations to thrive. She believes the only way this can happen is driven by the business sector.

Now back in the UK, Linda is a *Leadership Coach*, based west of London. She works with business clients who have big visions to change the world for the better. Using non-linear tools and methods, Linda specialises in helping clients connect with their deep purpose and drivers for success to make the big change happen.

If you have any questions or would like some help using these tools contact Linda at:

linda@lindaduff.com

www.lindaduff.com

Three simple steps for becoming your best self and creating your best life

Robert Wilcocks

*"Ever more people today have the means to live,
but no meaning to live for."*

Viktor Frankl

Most entrepreneurs and those associated with start-ups imagine riches, security and freedom, but the journey of entrepreneurship is not a straight line from start-up to success. It is a bumpy roller coaster with many highs and lows throughout the ride.

Many entrepreneurs, at some point, run into a challenge, if not a crisis, of meaning and purpose.

The answer is to look within, to think more deeply about your goals, values, and aspirations and to self-leadership.

It is not easy to do this effectively and so, I have created a three-step method called, *Dream, Vision and Act* (DVA), which is a framework designed to help entrepreneurs gain clarity and focus by finding greater meaning and purpose. Anyone can use this method to help them get the life and the business they really want.

This is also the method I use with in my financial planning business to help design their dream life and craft a financial plan that align to that vision.

I use *DVA* in my *Entrepreneurial Wealth Management* business, to help my clients design their dream life and to craft a financial plan that allows them to achieve it.

DVA is easy to follow; it is fun; it frees you up to discover your best life and, most importantly, it works!

Let's take a quick look at the structure of the *DVA Method:*

Dream

If you want a dream life you must allow yourself to dream. A dream is unconstrained. Allow your feelings around family, creativity, spirituality, community, business, philanthropy, and anything else to expand. This is blue sky thinking with a structure to help.

Vision

For your dreams to be realised, you must have a clear vision of what success looks like. In *Vision*, we use the power of stories to create a motivating vision of the future. What life will look like a year; three years; five years from now. What about ten years from now? Have you got a compelling vision for your future? Does it excite you? Is it important enough that you must succeed?

Act

The third step is that you must act. This requires prioritising your goals and setting plans for overcoming obstacles. This section provides a structure, along with examples, of how to overcome procrastination and act each day to achieve your vision.

Now it is time to play the *DVA Games!*

Part 1: Dreaming and Dream Games

*"Whatever the mind can conceive and believe,
the mind can achieve"*

Napoleon Hill

To help you design your dream life I have created a tool called *Dream Games* that allows you to dream!

The *Dream Games* are based on the works of people like *George Kinder, Bill Bacharach* and *Paul Armson*– mentors who have helped shape my firm's approach to wealth management. In addition, we draw on the work of *Abraham Harold Maslow* and *Viktor Frankl*. These masters have laid the groundworks for us all to better think about and articulate our goals, values, and aspirations for the future, such that we find meaning and purpose in life.

Here are a few of *Dream Games* you can try out:

1. The Lottery Game

Imagine that you wake up tomorrow and you have won the lottery! You never have to worry about money again.

Describe what an abundant, complete life looks like to you.

Do not hold back.

2. Doctor When

Imagine that you were told by *Dr When* that you were going to die - in ten years' time. You won't feel sick, but you do know when your time is up.

Knowing that you have only ten years left, your doctor asks you what you are going to do with the remaining time. What changes, if any, would you make now?

(You have your current financial resources).

3. The Crystal Ball

Imagine that you are aged 90, sitting in your comfy armchair in your old people's home. The nurse tells you that you will not feel any pain, but you will not wake up when you put your head on the pillow tonight. As you sit there staring out of the window, you reflect on any opportunities missed; places you did not go; things you did not achieve; the person you did not become.

Coming back to the present day, what would you miss the most about your future, if today was your last day on earth?

The answers will get to the core of what matters most to you, so you can make better life decisions.

4. The Money-Values Pyramid

The Money-Values Pyramid game draws on Maslow's *Hierarchy of Needs* theory. You will create a pyramid of your goals and values. The idea is you start with foundations and base needs at the bottom and end with your highest values at the top.

To start, draw a large pyramid and split it into horizontal rectangles. Ask yourself, "Why is money important to me?" Write your answer in the bottom rectangle.

Let's call your answer X. Next ask yourself, "Why is X important to me?" Write the answer to that question above the last one.

Then ask, "And why is that important?"

Add as many steps as you need.

This will help you to grow and maintain a positive relationship with money, as you solidify why money is important. This might help stop frivolous spending or encourage savings towards life goals which leads to greater freedom.

Part Two: Your Vision

"When you cease to dream, you cease to live."
Malcolm Forbes

Now that you have dreamt far and wide about the life you want, you can start to turn this into a *Vision* that will compel and drive you to *Act*.

To do this, you need to drill down into all the goals from *Dream* and attempt to create a joined-up picture of your *Dream Life*.

Here's the process I use to help my clients create their *Vision*:

Step One: Drill-Down

Take the goals and objectives identified in the *Dream Games* and start with the goal you feel is most important to you.

- "Tell me more about X?"
- "Why is X important to you?"
- "Is there anything else about X?"

The most important thing when drilling down into your goals, values and aspirations, is that you consider your answers without judging yourself. Importantly, listen to yourself and stay present. Your emotions and gut will tell you what is most important.

Step Two: Describe

Taking the goals from Drill-Down, your job is now to vividly describe your Dream Life back to yourself in a story format.

Join your goals up into your perfect day. Where do you live? Who are you with? What are you doing? How does it make you feel?

Go as far as you can with your story and describe your perfect week, month, and so on. Use a mirror if it helps.

Tips

- The shorter the timeframe the better. Yet, if some goals seem too 'big', don't fret. The timeframe needs to be realistic but not too far away. Anywhere from 1-36 months, depending on the goal, is good.

- Take the time to pause throughout the telling of your story. Let the feelings and emotions sink in. The feelings created here by the vivid description of outcomes (goals, dreams) are the energy that fuels action later. "Let the pause be with you."

- At the end of the story ask yourself, "Is there anything missing from this picture?"

Step Three: Dictate

Once you have finished drilling down into the goals and painted a vivid description of your Dream Life, the next step is to write it down in letter format.

Now write a detailed letter to a trusted friend, mentor, advisor or coach and forward date it a year or two away. You will be writing as your future self; describing how the last couple of years has been. Describe a life that is now rich, fulfilling and truly yours.

When done, read the letter back to your current self. How does it make you feel? How would it be to have accomplished all that is in your letter? This emotion is your rocket fuel!

Tips

- Do not hold back – this is the vision of your *Dream Life*, not your average life, after all.

- If you prefer speaking to writing, you could use an App like *Rev.com* which professionally transcribes your words into writing.

Part Three: ACT

"What is not started will never get finished."
J.W. Von Goethe

You have already worked out what you want and why it is so important to you.

Your brain has told you what you need to do to achieve your goals, become your best self and live your best life.

If you do this exercise you:

- May start to put up barriers and obstacles to your own success.
- Equally, you might start to think about the necessary actions to achieve your goals. Great!
- Or, you may have a combination of both of the above.

The question that remains is: how do you get out of your present situation, and take the necessary steps to find your best self and your best life?

Having worked for many years advising wealthy entrepreneurs and senior executives, I have noticed that what sets the really successful ones apart is that they make decisions quickly and then they can act! They are not afraid to fail. They are afraid of wasting time!

Successful people set goals, starting with the end in mind and identifying the outcome they want. Then, they *reverse engineer* the steps required to reach their goals.

You might be daunted by the problems and obstacles that

could get in your way and be tempted to do nothing. The key here is that successful people ACT! Having a dream and a vision is not enough.

- Aged 41, Mel Robbins was an unemployed journalist, stuck in a downward spiral and going in the opposite direction to her *Dream Life*.
  Things were not ideal and she was feeling despondent and discouraged.
  After doing this activity, she knew what her *Dream Life* looked like, which included being a better wife, mum, friend and person. She was able to create a clear vision to move forward; she even identified action steps.
  However, Mel could not get past the obstacles in her head and she was not taking the necessary daily steps to take her away from pain, towards happiness. She was stuck in a negative pattern of behaviour and thinking
  Then, one morning she saw a documentary about the NASA space program and she thought, "That is it! I am going to launch myself out of bed as if I am a NASA rocket!" She counted down aloud, 5, 4, 3, 2, 1 and catapulted herself out of bed.
  She realised that she had found a way to face reality, outsmart her own brain and take action.

- James Stockdale was a US Fighter pilot shot down over Vietnam during the war. He was held as a prisoner of war in the infamous *Hanoi Hilton* prison for over seven and a half years.
  James Collins, the author, interviewed Stockdale and asked him how he was able to cope with daily torture and living in a 3 x 6 foot cell for over seven years?
  "I never lost faith in the end of the story, I never doubted, not only that I would get out, but also, that I would prevail in the end and turn the experience into the defining event of my life which, in retrospect, I would not trade".

Stockdale's story demonstrates that it helps, when the going gets tough, to make sure your goals are connected to your values and ultimate life plan. Having a deeper meaning and purpose, "Your ultimate life plan" is the fuel to keep you going when things are difficult.

Both Mel Robbins and Stockdale fought through the demons and kept going day by day towards their goals.

Their experiences demonstrate that it is not enough to simply do the *Dream* and *Vision* stages of the exercise. You have to take decisive action and have faith in the journey and the outcome and, above all, keep going

Remember to *Dream*.

Create your compelling *Vision*.

Act.

References

- Kinder, G (2006). *Lighting The Torch: The Kinder Method (TM) of Life Planning*. FPA Press

- Maslow, A.H. (1943). *A theory of human motivation*. Psychological Review. 50 (4): 370–96.

- Collins, J. C. (2001). *Good to great: why some companies make the leap ... and others don't*. New York, NY, Harper Business.

- Bacharach, B (2000). *Values-Based Financial Planning: The Art of Creating and Inspiring Financial Strategy. Aim High Publishing.*

- Robbins, M & Bilyeu, T: *The Secret to Self-Motivation* https://www.youtube.com/watch?v=2Lz0VOItZKA&t=7s

Robert Wilcocks is a Wealth Manager and Registered Life Planner. He is also the Co-founder of *Wilcocks & Wilcocks*, and has been featured in *The Times* and *The Telegraph* in the top 1%, and the top 250, wealth managers in the UK.

Robert advises successful entrepreneurs and families to plan ahead and take control of their life and retirement goals. He uses his CLEARER framework which is about listening first, planning second, and implementing advice third – once he really knows and understands his client's goals, values and aspirations.

CLEARER takes clients on a journey that invests their money using over six decades of Nobel prize winning academic research, reduces their tax liabilities, strips out the risk in their personal and business lives, and ultimately delivers the wealth that they have worked tirelessly to build to their children and benefactors safely and tax efficiently.

In short, he makes his clients financially bulletproof. He gives them peace of mind about their financial future, and more time to get on with the job of running their businesses and living a great life.

Robert's mission is to work with entrepreneurs and families to help them protect and grow their capital, and get a great return on life.

www.wilcocksandwilcocks.co.uk

Best-Practice

Performance, productivity, efficacy, effectiveness, efficiency, fast-tracking, current best thinking, compliance, governance, due diligence

Collaborative Leadership

Kim Newman

When I started work my first job was as a Trainee Surveyor for a construction consultancy. Back in the 80's you couldn't find a more male dominated or traditional working environment where you sat one side of a table and a contractor sat on the other and the *Master and Slave* adversarial culture was well and truly embedded.

When things went wrong it was definitely someone's fault and someone was to blame and your manager made a point of telling you, sometimes at length! Behaviours were rarely regulated and were certainly not always appropriate.

Customers were a necessary evil and were not always right and they got an 'off the shelf' service, your focus was achieving productivity targets and fee recovery rates, we didn't have time to speak to clients let alone co-create a bespoke solution.

What an example to experience at the beginning of your career! The term *collaboration* definitely hadn't been invented let alone the behaviours to support it but I knew that there was another way.

Having now run my own business for over 20 years built on the principles of collaboration, and having experienced the challenges of growing and running a business, I can happily say that there definitely is another way and actually, I think it is the only way to run a business. To use *Collaborative Leadership*.

What if, all the members of a senior management team or project team were on the same wavelength from day 1? What if they all shared a common understanding of the business or project objective(s) and were all clear about what a successful outcome for the business or a project would be?

What if they were all clear about what they expected of each other and understood what the others expected of them?

What if all key stakeholders could communicate with each other in a common language which made clear how they were feeling?

What if everyone in the team felt able to give and receive open and honest feedback and use this feedback constructively to continually improve their performance and the success of the business or project as a whole?

What if the team benchmarked their performance, proactively sought to find win:win solutions and felt empowered to resolve any disputes quickly and objectively as they arise?

All of this requires outstanding collaboration by the leader and between key stakeholders within the team. In turn, outstanding collaboration requires everyone to exhibit collaborative behaviours.

If all this were possible, teams working in collaboration could achieve results faster, complete projects faster, cheaper and to the same or higher quality, reduce waste and add value. They could reduce the number of disputes, increase innovation and continually improve the way that they do things resulting in more satisfied customers and a higher level of satisfaction.

A key factor in implementing collaborative leadership is to acknowledge that we don't always know what collaboration means or how to implement it in practice, we don't know what we don't know. Likewise, becoming a leader doesn't come with an automatic set of skills, collaboration doesn't come naturally to everyone either. It's not enough for leaders to spot collaborative opportunities. They must also set the tone by being good collaborators themselves.

Collaboration has also unfortunately become an overused term in some sectors, used frequently as a fashionable term but without the understanding or behaviours to back it up. This often means that the key ingredients of successful collaborative leadership are often overlooked.

Part of the problem is that many leadership teams, composed of the CEO and his or her direct reports, actually don't often operate as teams. Each member runs his or her own region, function, or product or service category, without much responsibility—or incentive—for aligning the organisation's various projects and operations into a coherent whole. Silo mentality takes hold. Teams typically believe issues belong to the other team, department or organisation.

None of us is as smart as all of us. When people recognise their own erroneous beliefs, and work together to change them silos are broken down.

Some of the most successful organisations promote a collaborative mind-set at all levels. It is not unusual for competing agendas to exist among senior managers which then begins to threaten a company's potential due to the lack of alignment.

When we work with organisations to embed a collaborative approach each senior manager embarks on a *personal journey*, we work as a trainer and coach and meet with everyone individually and with the team as a group. It is a very different type of approach. It's not just talking to your boss or subordinates; it is more holistic, broader, integrating all the different roles.

Quite often this can lead to managers making themselves vulnerable, showing that they are not supermen, that they have failures; that they are afraid of some things and we don't have all the answers. The sort of difficult conversations that generally don't tend to happen.

Once the collaborative mind-set has been embedded at the top this is then typically cascaded down to the rest of the organisation, and the process is rolled out to all the company's managers with reviews and check in points scheduled.

Refocusing senior managers so that they are rewarded for collaborating rather than promoting their individual agendas is absolutely essential.

Once leaders really buy into collaboration and start getting employees to collaborate, a different problem often occurs: overdoing it. The tendency will be for people to try to collaborate on everything resulting in endless meetings, constantly debating ideas, finding it impossible to find consensus of opinion. They can't reach decisions and implement quickly. Collaboration ceases to be the oil greasing the wheel and brings it to a grinding halt.

Effective collaborative leaders therefore need to assume a strong role directing teams. They will maintain agility by forming and disbanding them as opportunities come and go—in much the same way that project managers, contractors and designers establish teams for the life of a project. Collaborative activity is therefore highly flexible and is not confined to company silos.

Effective collaborative leaders also assign clear roles, responsibilities and decision-making powers so that at the appropriate point someone can bring a discussion to an end and make a final decision.

Differences in cultural values, and operating approaches inevitably add complexity to collaborative efforts. But they also make them richer, more innovative, and more valuable. Getting that value is the heart of collaborative leadership.

In my experience therefore, successful collaborative leaders exhibit the following properties:

- They build teams that have a clearly defined common goal that they are all committed to achieving together.

- They understand the expectations of them from their colleagues, staff and partners and vice versa.

- They define and agree a set of behaviours and abide by them.

- They understand the value of constructive feedback which is then used continually to improve performance

- Performance is benchmarked against best practice to continually gauge performance.

Ultimately though, by far the biggest success factor is the commitment and trust of the people involved to make things work. This might sound simple, but often a host of barriers have to be overcome before this can be achieved.

Barriers

- **Understanding how to behave collaboratively**
  This is not something that is often taught to leaders, managers or professionals, despite the fact that many of us spend most of our working lives working in collaborative teams of one sort or another.

- **The giving and receiving of feedback**
  If you are not used to receiving feedback, particularly if it questions knowledge, approach, ideas or efficiency, personal perceptions can feel like a personal attack, resulting in defensive and un-cooperative behaviour. Alternatively, if feedback is received as a gift, presenting opportunities to refine and improve performance, it is much more likely to be viewed positively, resulting in constructive, creative and co-operative behaviour. Similarly, the giving of open and honest feedback is much more likely if the giver knows that it will be received as a gift rather than personal attack.

- **Encouraging all parties to participate**
  Some of the best ideas come from staff and teams working *at the coal face* that are often not asked for their opinion or input. Often the simplest of solutions are the best ones, creating an environment where great solutions can be shared equally by all involved is a key objective for a collaborative leader who wishes to develop high performing collaborative teams.

I passionately believe that collaborative leadership is a massive source of efficiency, improved creativity and increased predictability for high performing teams. That is why, as a business, we have invested considerable time and effort, over a number of years, to research and develop a programme of collaborative behavioural training for leaders and multi-party teams who learn and develop together.

We focus on defining a common goal that all parties sign up to. All parties learn about the importance of perceptions and feedback and how to give and receive feedback in a safe environment for the purpose of building mutual understanding.

This feedback is the foundation for performance improvement of all parties. We also share a *collaborative language* with all parties, which enables them to emphasise their intent and share how messages are being received. The outcome is much clearer communication, irrespective of the channel used.

Supporting this process is a method to measure how well the team are collaborating and help teams to focus on those tasks that are crucial for success and continuous improvement. Critical to this process is identifying lessons learnt at key milestones and agreeing how they will be shared.

Collaborative behavioural training has been successfully delivered to a wide range of leaders and their teams from all sectors across the UK. It is the nearest thing to a silver bullet that we've found in the collaborative training world. The outcomes achieved by truly collaborative teams can be transformational.

Kim Newman is an established business leader and business improvement specialist to the public and private sector and was awarded an entry in the *Who's Who of Britain's Business Elite* in 2009.

Kim has over 25 years experience having originally qualified as a surveyor and then progressed into a variety of roles with national consultancy practices.

Since 1996 she has been a co-owner of *PML*, a leading consultancy and advisory business that works with organisations and leaders to give them the skills to collaborate more effectively with their staff, teams and customers.

Kim is an adviser, trainer and coach and is passionate about great customer service and constantly looks for ways to improve and develop her business by working collaboratively with others.

Kim_newman@pmlgroup.com

www.pmlgroup.com

How Branding Helps You Communicate as a Leader

Sapna Pieroux

"Leadership requires two things: a vision of the world that does not yet exist and the ability to communicate it."
Simon Sinek

You're a leader. You've found your *why* and your purpose in life. You've developed an amazing product or service, started a company and you aim to give your customers a great experience.

You now need to tell people what you do in order to make a difference, so you spend time finding the best words to communicate your big message. You rehearse your pitch and tweak it until you can speak it with confidence – and others feel compelled to listen. You read books, listen to speakers, learn from the business greats, maybe even hire a coach. You network, blog, vlog, tweet … maybe even write a book (or a chapter of one…)

Your image is also important. First impressions matter. People make decisions about you within the first six seconds. So you invest money, time and commitment in health and fitness, not just so you are strong and fit to lead, but also (admit it) so you *look the part*. You spend on the right clothes, accessories, products, technology, photography and videography. You may even invest in a gym, stylists, treatments, trainers, dermatologists, surgeons. Come on, you do check your teeth for spinach before a meeting…?!

At the very least, all this effort means that nothing detracts from your message. A client once told me she knew I could do wonders for her branding because of the way I was *'put together'* so it can even help you win business.

When you *look the business*, people respond accordingly.

But have you put as much thought, effort and investment into your company branding? And what does branding mean anyway?

Many business owners talk about their *branding* when they mean their logo. The term *branding* comes from the days when cattle were burned with a hot iron *brand* to denote which farmer they belonged to. Nowadays, though, your brand and branding should go more than skin deep.

In short, your brand is the sum of everything you do as a company. Branding is how you communicate this.

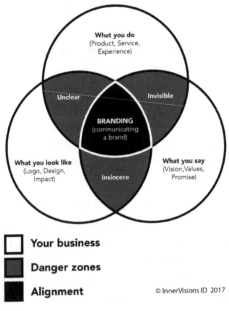

In an increasingly visual world, branding is about strategically aligning everything you do and your communications with your image.

As a leader, your corporate branding should act as your 'silent ambassador', helping you communicate your goals, values and vision.

Great branding doesn't just give a favourable impression of your company, it should also give it a personality, communicate your promise, tell your story, amplify your message, help make the right associations and connect with your audience – all before you even show up.

As the diagram shows, branding should be core to all parts of your business to communicate your purpose with clarity.

The three dangers lie in not giving equal importance to what your company does, what you communicate and how it looks:

- **Insincere:** If your company looks great and promises the world but then fails to deliver, you will disappoint your customers.

- **Unclear:** If you have a great-looking website and a product or service to match but you can't communicate the value of what you do nor who you do it for, then your potential customers will be confused.

- **Invisible:** If you have a great product or service, and all the right words, but your business card, brochure and website look terrible, you will not stand out against your competitors

So, is your branding helping with - or detracting from – your purpose?

Branding in business strategy

Often seen as a non-essential cost, branding should be considered as one of the most powerful components of your business strategy. Meaningful investment in this area can add considerable value and a real point of difference to your company, whatever its size.

Even if you are starting out, great branding is like dressing for the job you want, not the one you have.

It's worth investing in a professional to help you with your branding. They should ask lots of questions about your company to understand your vision and goals, help you analyse the branding of companies you aspire to, find out what you like, what you don't (and why!) to eventually create your corporate identity.

With a new brand, don't try and be over-clever. Whilst your branding may work on several levels, it shouldn't need too much explaining by the designer as to why you should love or *get* it.

Yes, *Nike* might get away with just a *swoosh* or a *Just Do It*, but they have spent decades and billions to get to that level of recognition.

If your branding doesn't immediately appeal, resonate, speak to or connect with your audience, it could be the difference between getting a sale or not.

As designer Raymond Loewy said, *"Between two products equal in price, function and quality the one with the most attractive exterior will win."*

Loewy was talking about design rather than branding, but the same rules apply. However great branding is more than just about looking good; it should help and align with your business objectives and goals.

Apple is a great illustration of this. The 1990s saw technology getting better, faster and cheaper. Great for *Microsoft*, but

Apple, with its more expensive products (at the time only really used by designers) was struggling. Steve Jobs' solution was not to try and price-match the competition, but to work on *Apple's* branding with the *Think Different* campaign. Going back to our diagram, they aligned their already-great products with stylish visuals and creative copy: all beautifully clever, distinctive, simple and powerful.

This succeeded in increasing desirability and demand for their products, and indeed great branding has been a major factor in maintaining Apple's premium position ever since.

For a leader, branding represents your pitch when you are not in the room, and should be every bit as carefully considered as your spoken one.

Everything you put out there should be echoing, emphasising, consolidating and consistently helping to communicate your message and over time (as with any relationship) clarity and consistency will be key to building confidence, credibility and trust in your brand.

Your branding is an unwritten promise to be professional and respectful of your customer's time, attention and opinion. It will tell people whether to take you and your company seriously, whether you are a professional - or not.

Great branding also helps you tell your story and communicate your message and purpose to connect with people on an emotional level, building brand loyalty.

Brand fans and communities engender goodwill and trust for your brand. As Andrew Beattie writes, *"The power of branding can help a company triumph in a price war, thrive in a recession, or simply grow operating margins and create shareholder value. Like the brand itself, the premium that investors are willing to pay for the stock with a branding edge is almost entirely a psychological choice."*

Branding is an asset for your business. It can mean a return on investment of up to 30% although, intangible as the benefits often are, it's hard to give an exact figure. Still, something to consider within your exit strategy.

Brand and branding is why *Rolex, Mercedes* and *Chanel* can charge way above the sum of their component parts. When you invest in these brands you are not just buying a watch, car or bag - you are buying into a dream, a promise, a lifestyle, a *#lifegoal* - suddenly part of an elite group.

Even non-luxury brands like *Coca Cola, Perrier* and *Volkswagen* have all weathered controversies and come back stronger, because of the loyalty they have cultivated through their brand and branding.

Branding Elements

When developing your branding there are so many things to consider. These are just a few, and we will demonstrate them through our case study.

Personality makes your brand stand out from the crowd. Is your brand formal? Friendly? Sophisticated? Brash? Make sure the written word aligns with your pitch and consider investing in bespoke photography or illustration to echo your brand personality and values.

Colours infer characteristics and are proven to influence buyer decisions (so don't just pick your favourites!), e.g. dark blue can convey authority, trust, establishment; red; power, strength; green: can be caring, natural or calming.

Typefaces again must not detract from, your message. Serifs look traditional, sans serifs look modern and each typeface has a personality. The wrong choice can diminish your message's legibility and credibility.

What would you think if a legal company's website was written in Comic Sans?!

Or you saw a high-tech company using this swirly typeface?!

Case study: Antoinette Oglethorpe

A specialist in leadership training in high-tech organisations, Antoinette Oglethorpe came to me in 2016 asking for a brochure design. However, I could see that her current logo, website and brochures were inconsistent and not speaking to her target market, nor did they reflect the eloquent, professional, clever and immaculately-groomed woman before me.

The short story was that she needed more than a brochure - as her first book (*Grow Your Geeks*) was coming out and her profile was about to rocket - she needed a rebrand.

Antoinette was understandably nervous of a complete change to all her collateral so close to launch. Besides, the book jacket had tested well, was already being promoted and we simply didn't have the time.

So we decided to reverse-engineer her new branding to go with her book jacket; going for evolution rather than revolution. We kept the logo shape the same so we could subtly replace the old one in existing collateral before a full redesign could take place.

Here's the *before:*

Antoinette's branding should have been a key part of how she could present herself and her company. To embody visually her professionalism to potential customers and to reflect their aspirations: modern, cutting-edge leadership techniques and solutions.

The original logo was largely fuchsia pink with a swirly script typeface. It looked girly and dated, not appropriate for her high-tech, contemporary audience.

The designer had accommodated Antoinette's love of jewel shades but they were the wrong colours for her business.

For the rebrand, we chose a sleek and modern san-serif typeface (Antoinette was delighted to discover it was in the same family as used by tech and business giants *Microsoft*, *Apple* and *LinkedIn*).

As her name is so long Antoinette wanted to keep an *AO* rounded that could be used in isolation, but we brought symbolism and a story into it - the '*A*' representing a mountain, the '*O*' representing an individual ready to climb it (their rise to leadership).

We retained the jewel purple and the neutral grey from her original logo to maintain some familiarity but replaced the pink with a deep jade green, signifying growth and development. We ditched the cyan blue for the *AO*, but introduced a wider 'jewel' palette to take through the rest of her branding. We also made sure her strapline was working harder for her.

Here's the *after*:

Antoinette ⬡ Oglethorpe

DEVELOP LEADERS • DELIVER STRATEGY • DRIVE RESULTS

It's impossible to show the full effect of the colourful rebrand on these pages, but we've since rolled the full brand identity out over her stationery, website and various publications.

Antoinette was amazed at what this subtle but powerful makeover did for her and her business:

"I felt (the rebrand) enhanced my credibility … that my company has now 'grown up' and I am playing at a higher level.

"My brand is now aligned with who I am and what I am saying.

"It brings a sophistication and maturity to my collateral, an additional professionalism to everything. First impressions are stronger: clients have complimented me on how I present myself on paper.

"My branding adds another dimension and I feel I'm being offered new, more significant, opportunities as a result. It is easier to be confident selling a high-value package when it looks the part too."

So you see, branding, when aligned with your business strategy, can elevate even the simplest of concepts - a logo of your name - and instantly enhance your ability as a leader to look great and communicate more clearly.

To paraphrase Sinek: branding helps you with two things as a leader: a vision of the world that does not yet exist and the ability to communicate it.

References

- Beattie, Andrew, *The Power of Branding* www.investopedia.com

- The long, three-part story is on www.InnerVisions-ID.com/blog

Sapna Pieroux is an award-winning Brand Consultant and Design Coach.

Having studied Graphic Design, then Marketing, Sapna was immediately offered a marketing job in radio. Frustrated with their design agency, she set up an in-house agency for the radio group - and then their clients.

She freelanced for several design agencies before being lured back to radio, this time helping brands communicate creatively via promotions, sponsorships and events at *Chrysalis*, then *emap*.

Sapna moved into cross-media, managing large budgets and virtual sales teams, creatives, programmers and writers to come up with creative campaigns across *emap's* radio, TV, online, magazines, events and mobile platforms, for e.g. *Rimmel, Oakley, Selfridges, Toyota* and *Sony Ericsson*.

Headhunted by *The Telegraph* to do the same, she won several service, creativity and sales awards there, then went on to work for *Blyk* (a youth mobile network), *Trinity Mirror Group* and *O2 Media*. Her *Blyk 'Green Thing'* campaign won a *Mobile Effectiveness Award* and was used at *Harvard Business School* as a case study.

Sapna has now put 20+ years of design and brand communications experience into her own company. *InnerVisions ID* now helps ambitious entrepreneurs build their own brands and support their business goals by looking great and communicating more clearly.

She is also a Brand Mentor for the *Shifts to Success* programme *www.shiftstosuccess.com* and lives in London with her husband and two boys.

www.InnerVisions-ID.com

Twitter: @InnerVisionsID

Facebook: www.facebook.com/InnerVisionsID

Linked In: www.linkedin.com/in/sapnapieroux

Discover the surprising strategy to increase the conversion of your online advertising: A Not-So-Common Take On Leadership

Gaël Reignier

Numbers don't lie.

Black on white.

"Faster, Stronger and Higher".

This is how I define leadership: Performance.

In my opinion, leadership in business is ultimately measured by profits and the biggest influencer of profit is revenue (sales). (Costs are important, but managing costs won't bring new money).

- Why do businesses train staff? To increase productivity and revenue.

- Why do businesses want to connect with their clients? To sell more.

- Why do businesses offer great customer service? To retain business and increase revenue.

As a business leader, your success in sales depends on conversion at every step of your sales funnel. As you read what follows, you will discover how you can influence the conversion of your online advertising and lead your organisation to new heights.

The unusual conversion

If you were with me when I was 14 years old, you would have witnessed something extraordinary. My dad, standing by the doors of our clothes shop, speaking with people who did not buy, to ultimately usher them back in to find them 30 minutes later with a shopping basket overflowing with neat shirts, suits and shoes…

I never saw anyone else doing that. Having the ability to grab the attention of a prospect, in such a way that they went back into the shop and spent hundreds of Euros.

Well …

My dad owned one vital skill. He was a master converter. He spoke to them the way they wanted to be spoken to. He tested and refined his approach over 40 years. And, more importantly, he used the right words. Today, conversion happens online.

Online advertising is not so simple…

Unfortunately, like many small and medium size businesses advertising online, you might be bleeding 'ads money' every day of the month.

As word of mouth marketing could only grow your business so far, online advertising looked like the Holy Grail with its amazing promise: "Pay to advertise; get clients."

Until … you realise that you don't have the results you want: few people click on your ad and fewer take action.

If you feel discouraged or disheartened, then I am here to tell you …

Your prayers for better conversion have already been answered; you just don't know it yet. You probably think that fighting the ad battle is unfair. After all, the audience has an ever-shortening attention span and you compete against businesses with large ad budgets.

Despite having the right campaign, targeting the right audience, buying the right keywords; there is one strategy for effective ads' campaigns that is missing.

One insider secret to increase conversion. Imagine getting more clicks on your ads, more downloads of your lead magnet and ultimately ... more people to buy from you!

Today, I will share this secret strategy with you. However ...

To be effective, strategies must be applied. This is why I will reveal three ways to implement it, to increase conversion, and ultimately get more clients. Why do I do that? Because I fight what I call: *Toxic Advertising.*

It is advertising that hurts the business and the clients. I saw it first-hand when my dad fell victim to it. He has been sold poor displays with atrocious advice, costing him thousands and I want to avoid that happening to you. So, buckle up and let's dive into it.

First, I would like you to picture your online advertising as made of two parts:

1. The engine; and
2. The gas.

The **engine** is the distribution of the ads. I will use *Facebook,* because it became ubiquitous. The **gas** is the copy of your ad.

Now I will unveil something only few people know.

Why do people buy from you?

When faced with poor conversion, people focus on the engine: they tweak the audience, change the advertising objective or create special offers. Even though it helps, it is only treating the symptoms of poor conversion. You can have the best engine in the world; you get the best performance when using the right gas. And the most impactful strategy, the gasoline of online advertising, is the copy.

Copy is selling in print.

Imagine having a sales rep that NEVER sleeps and improves day after day.

The copy will be tweaked and refined, while using the same "engine." Online, you get feedback rapidly. You can test and choose the best copy in a couple of days.

However, I refer to a specific type of copy: **Direct-Response** copywriting.

The ultimate goal of Direct-Response is to put money in your wallet. It is done by gaining an intimate understanding of your audience and its buying psychology. Answering the question: "Why do people buy from me?"

The first objective is to adapt your copy to engage your audience in the way it wants to be engaged.

This is grounded in the **Level of Awareness** of your audience.

Today, you will discover how to successfully address clients at the *Level 2 of Awareness*.

How does the Level of Awareness impact your business?

Unfortunately, most businesses speak with their audience in only one way. Nothing wrong with that, when they sell through word of mouth (Level 1 of awareness). You would hear them say:

"I will tell them what I have done. If they want it, they buy it. And if they don't, I will find someone else who wants it."

It worked, because the audience already Knows, Likes and Trusts them. It comprises of the friends, family and existing clients. However, when you enter the world of online advertising ...

The audience does not know you yet.

You must adapt to survive. If you don't, you will leave money on the table day after day because you have not adapted to the level of awareness of your audience. Thankfully, metrics helps you monitor your performance. The four key metrics are:

- **Click Through Rate (CTR):** Percentage of people who clicked on your ad;
- **Cost Per Click (CPC):** Cost of each click on your ad;
- **Conversion Rate (CVR):** Percentage of people who take action on the page after your ad;
- **Cost Per Acquisition (CPA):** Cost of each person who took action.

To give you a performance benchmark, *Wordstream* conducted a study of 256 US-based *Facebook Advertising* campaigns and here are the average results across industries:

- **CTR:** 0.90%
- **CPC:** $1.72
- **CVR:** 9.21%
- **CPA:** $18.68

It's great when you hit these metrics! However, let's beat the average and increase your CTR and VCR, while reducing your CPC and CPA using copy.

What is the Level of Awareness and how to use it?

This is a fundamental concept to advertise efficiently and generate more sales. Eugene Schwartz, the advertising legend, coined it in his book: *Breakthrough Advertising. The Level of Awareness* is the third pillar of the methodology I created: the

Four Pillars of Growth. To easily understand it, I will compare the *Level of Awareness* to a relationship.

Imagine you are on your first date with your future partner for life. During the dinner, you will want to know more about the person, where they live, what their job is, what they love in life … Now, fast-forward 20 years. You are happily married with kids. Imagine during dinner you ask the EXACT same questions …

I will let that sink in for a moment.

Of course you would not. The awareness of each other has evolved over the past 20 years! You would talk about what is relevant in your new context: home, kids, holidays…

The same applies in business: you **must** adapt your marketing copy to the awareness your audience has of **your business** and **your offers.**

The levels of awareness applied to business

Every person who is in a market has a problem to solve. However, not everyone knows how to solve the problem and who can solve it. There are five levels of awareness:

- **Level 1:** People who know **you;**
- **Level 2:** People aware of **solutions;**
- **Level 3:** People aware of their **problem;**
- **Level 4:** People aware of their **desire;**
- **Level 5:** People **not aware** of their needs.

The objective is to go up through the levels, one at a time.

Let us look at the thinking process of a couple that expect their first child and need a new car. I will focus on Levels 4 to 1, as they are the most commonly used.

Levels of Awareness

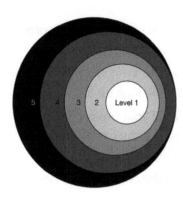

Level 1: People who know you
They are existing clients
Objective: Present your offer

Level 2: Solution Aware
Objective: Show them why you offer
the best solution

Level 3: Problem Aware
Objective: Show them that you offer
a potential solution

Level 4: Desire Aware
Objective: Help them by articulating
their problem

Level 5: Totally unaware
Objective: Define their desire

Level 4: They know that they have a new **need** to satisfy; they need to transport their growing family. It was not on their *radar* before and now, they need to do something about it. This is when they start their *quest* to fulfill a new need.

Level 3: They are clear about the **problem** they want to solve: "I need a new car and I need buy a baby seat and a pushchair." They have done **researching online** and discovered solutions: they know which cars are available, which one would work best and they have shortlisted some options.

Level 2: They are about to make a decision. They know the available solutions however, they are still hesitant to make a purchase decision. They must be convinced.

What to tell people at Level 2 of Awareness?

Considering it is a family car, safety is important and I will use it as an example. Out of the seven ways to engage a prospect at Level 2, the five most important are:

- Give a strong promise using a **new mechanism** to satisfy it i.e., Technologies like ABS, ESP or Lane Departure Warning…

- Add a new **proof** that demonstrates your claim such as news, research, or endorsement i.e., The car won a *Car Safety Award*.

- Reinforce the **desire** the person has to own your product and get the outcome. i.e., Show a happy family.

- **Extend the image** of the reader. Who will they become? i.e., Become the dad that people look up to.

- Sharpen the **mental picture** of your product i.e., Describe how it feels to drive the car, often done during TV shows, in magazines ...

Now that we know what to put in the ad, let us see how to find out what works best.

Keep testing

The next step to increase conversion is to keep testing. The Internet has made it EXTREMELY simple to test advertising and adjust very quickly. Ask yourself this question: *"How many different version of the same ad am I running right now?"*

Look. Marketing is about discovering what the market wants by understanding how it reacts to your offering. It is very simple however, it is often overlooked. There are five steps to follow:

1. Create two ads
2. Dedicate a small budget to each one
3. After 1,000 impressions, declare a winner
4. Run the winning ad
5. Later on, beat the winner.

Now, let us see how to create a high-converting ad with these three copy rules.

Three rules for great conversion

Time to write the ad! You know which elements to put in your new ad (using the Level of Awareness).What follows are the three most important components to create it:

1. **Use a benefit driven headline.** *What's In It For Them*: What's the big benefit of your offer. Exercise: show the transformation they will get.

2. **Write client-centric content.** Talk about *Them* and how your offer will change their life for the better. Exercise: count the number of times you use *I/Mine* and *You/Your*. You should have more *you* than *I*.

3. **Use a strong Call To Action.** The action you want them to take must be crystal clear. The more specific, the better, even if it sounds too obvious. Do the thinking for them and you will increase your chances of conversion. *Exercise:* Write an over detailed Call To Action.

Ready to increase your conversion?

As we have seen, the strategy to increase your conversion of your online ads, is to write copy that resonates with your audience and how to do it for a *Level 2 of Awareness*. Go ahead and follow these three steps to increase the conversion of your online ads:

- Adapt to the level of awareness of your audience
- Test your ad and declare a winner
- Use the three rules for great conversion

As my dad said: "Clients are always right, you just have to listen to them and give them what they want."

References

- Schwartz, Eugene. (2004), *Breakthrough Advertising,* Bottom Line Book

- Wordstream FB ads benchmark http://www.wordstream.com/blog/ws/2017/02/28/facebook-advertising-benchmarks

Gaël Reignier is a direct-response copywriter, who specialises in helping businesses to increase their conversion rate to sell more, by using his unique *RCD* methodology.

From a very young age he was in a sales environment, as his parents ran their businesses from home, before owning shops where he spent his time dealing with customers and selling to them (when he was not studying). This experience taught him that what is most important in business, is to walk the proverbial mile in the shoes of his clients.

As he worked for some of the greatest IT companies in the world, he sent over 20,000 emails over a period of four years to build relationships and to serve and grow his client portfolio.

Today, he combines his passion and experience to help businesses selling online programmes, expert public speakers and coaches grow their businesses.

http://www.gaelreignier.com

hello@gaelreignier.com

LinkedIn: http://bit.ly/linkedingael

Facebook: http://bit.ly/facebookgael

The 7 Step Blueprint for Agile Business Performance

Ian Thomas

Why should you read this? At school I enjoyed chemistry, so I sought and won a sponsorship from *Courtaulds* to study textile chemistry at *The University of Leeds*.

Like many at the tender age of 21, after graduating I didn't really know what I wanted to do with my life, but the sponsorship provided an R&D job as a research chemist so that's what I did.

I hated it!

I realised that I was not an R&D person, so I swapped the laboratory and test tubes for the multi-national, cross-functional challenge of marketing and managing the flagship product of International Paint (the market leading global marine paint company) - I never looked back.

I stayed with them for 18 years progressing through roles in sales, marketing, technical and commercial operations and steadily rose through the ranks to become the global marketing director for the marine division.

During that time, I received a first-class grounding in international business. I learned about strategy and how key business functions interact in successful companies. I learned that a strategy was only as good as its execution and effective execution needed employees to work together as a team towards a common goal.

I worked at building the skills to communicate, align and motivate teams to deliver large and complex projects and I became known for it.

I moved to *Castrol* to lead a restructuring of part of its European business and when *BP* bought *Castrol*, I led large post-merger integration projects before moving on to rationalise the European product range and then transform the global supply chain.

I have a passion for and a skill at marrying clear strategy with the teamwork behaviours necessary to deliver successful outcomes and I have incorporated everything I have experienced and everything I know into a *7 Step Blueprint* which you can follow to deliver successful outcomes in your business too.

Introduction

To achieve high performance and sustained success, businesses must embrace change. Whilst obvious for organisations in need of rapid turnaround, businesses which are performing well still need to be pro-active in keeping ahead in their marketplace. Simply put, there is never any justification to coast!

In our experience, organisations optimise their performance most effectively when they adopt a two-stage process of first identifying and addressing short-term, tactical changes, and then developing a longer-term strategic path towards business excellence. When working with clients, our interventions usually start by identifying quick-win improvements to uncover problems and opportunities that can be dealt with rapidly to get some *runs on the board* and add value quickly. The reason this approach is so impactful is simple: these initial successes strengthen organisational confidence and provide important time for reflection, which means that Leadership arrive at developing a more strategic approach feeling ready to consider the longer-term view.

When developing the longer-term strategy, perfecting the technical elements (e.g. marketing, operations and finance) is no guarantee of success. Equal value must be placed on addressing organisational health and refining the teamwork elements of strategy (e.g. people engagement, behaviours and culture). Both elements are essential for sustained success. As such, at the heart of our model is the development of a winning culture.

We work with clients in three stages:

- **Reviewing the Business**
  We identify short-term, value-adding changes using the 4 zone model (Figure 1, p134).

- **Building a Winning Culture**
  We advise on how to cultivate an environment which supports a cohesive teamwork culture.

- **Setting the Longer-Term Strategy: The Seven Step Blueprint**
  We work with the organisation to execute the short-term changes already identified, and set a longer-term strategy for agile business performance. We do this through guiding all levels of the organisation through seven key questions (see Table 1 p138).

Reviewing the Business

When we review a client's business, we analyse four key areas: *Marketing and Sales; Management, Administration and HR; Operations;* and *Financial Control.* Together, these form the *Change Zone,* as this is where all potential business developments take place.

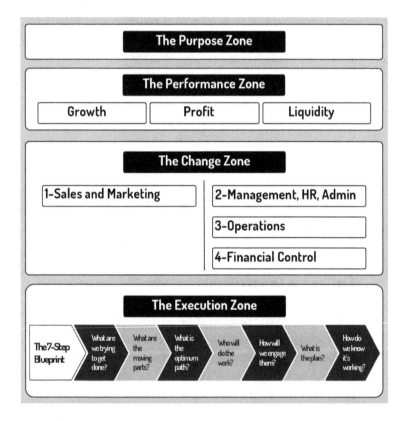

Figure 1. Model showing the four Zones: (from the top) Purpose, Performance, Change and Execution.

We identify areas with either problems that need addressing and/or opportunities to move the business forward, through asking targeted questions such as those below:

Sales and Marketing

- Does the business focus on a clearly defined target customer?
- Is sales activity enough to produce the desired revenue?

Operations

- Do we have sufficient resources to fulfil the sales developed by the sales and marketing team?
- Are there bottlenecks in the process that can be removed?

HR

- Are line managers modelling the way the business wants them to behave?
- Are we overseeing an employee engagement program to make sure our team are motivated and on-point throughout the employee life cycle?

Management

- Are they aware of the challenges and issues in the business?
- Are they making the appropriate interventions to correct?

Financial Control

- Do we know the cash position and cash-flow forecast?
- Do we have an ongoing handle on growth, profit and liquidity?

The Change Zone review arrives at several change options. We provide vital external challenge to help Leadership evaluate the impact of each proposed change option on the *Performance*

Zone and check alignment with organisational purpose in the *Purpose Zone*. The *Performance Zone* is comprised of business:

- Growth in terms of revenue
- Profitability in terms of net profit
- Liquidity: the amount of cash in the business and the cash-flow implications of the forward business plan.

As you can see in Figure 1, *Sales and Marketing* is the only *Change Zone* function that produces revenue. *Operations, Management, HR, Admin and Financial Control* are the essential costs of doing business.

Clearly a healthy business needs to have greater revenues than costs, so it is vital to evaluate each change option on the net impact of revenue and costs (profitability), increase in revenues (growth) of the business and the cash position (liquidity).

We recommend that a business prioritises and focuses on the single most important change goal at any one time.

This ensures that all resources are focused on the same project across the whole organisation.

Building a Winning Culture

Laying the foundations for a winning culture to flourish is prerequisite to attaining sustainable business success.

In our experience, a winning formula for organisational health is comprised of three elements:

- Clarity of organisational vision and purpose, well communicated by a cohesive and aligned leadership team
- A teamwork culture in terms of behaviours, attitudes and values

- Middle managers who are trained and equipped to support and coach their front-line teams to be successful.

In businesses where these conditions do not exist:

- The leadership team are not aligned and instead they pursue their individual and departmental agendas.
- Their teams become frustrated as they see other departments are not on the same page. A culture of departmental silo behaviour results and interdepartmental rivalry and internal politics raises its ugly head.
- Middle managers and their teams get sucked in to unwinnable inter-departmental battles.

Building a winning culture requires commitment from the leadership team, and a disciplined approach. When working with clients, we advise on how to fully embed this formula through implementation of the *7 Step Blueprint*.

The 7 Step Blueprint

The *7 Step Blueprint* challenges the organisation to answer seven clear and on the face of it, simple questions. We facilitate and challenge this at each level in the organisation to bring out the clarity, connection and meaning required.

Table 1 below gives an outline of each of the seven steps and how we use them at different levels in the organisation:

Step	Leadership	Middle Management	Front Line
#1 What are we trying to get done?	Agree purpose and vision. Set clear strategy and priorities. Communicate this effectively.	Interpret the strategy. Communicate to their teams how the strategy impacts their roles.	Understand the impact of their role in relation to the big picture. Gain clarity on their remit and focus.
#2 What are the moving parts?	Evaluate the organisation's available assets and options to organise them in the most effective way.	Determine the people and resources required for their teams to deliver.	Understand how they add value and how their work meshes with other functions.
#3 What is the optimum path?	Reach clarity on the best way to meet the organisation's targets and priorities, addressing departmental barriers if required.	Navigate interactions across departments and broker agreements where needed.	Understand what is required of them and how this relates to other functions, to deliver the overall strategy.
#4 Who is going to do the work?	Ensure the most effective allocation of teams, treating resources as fluid to avoid "departmental grab".	Ensure that their teams are properly resourced and have the right skill set, behaviours and attitude.	Be placed within optimum teams, based on skill set, behaviours and attitude.

Step	Leadership	Middle Management	Front Line
#5 How will we engage them?	Facilitate a quarterly strategy review to check on assumptions, performance and external factors. Adjust priorities accordingly. Check they are aligned and modelling 'the desired behaviours'	Develop leadership and coaching skills. Develop the skills required to interpret and communicate the strategy and model 'team-work behaviours' to their teams.	Understand organisational purpose, values and priorities. Be delegated intent not tasks. Own their bit. Feel supported to deliver their goals. Receive coaching on the 'required behaviours'
#6 What is the plan?	Deliver the strategy as set and adjusted quarterly with the agreed main current priority.	Deliver the current business priority through engaging their teams to build a detailed, resourced plan showing the critical path and dependencies.	Own their part in a detailed, well-resourced plan showing desired outcomes, clear accountabilities and critical path.

Step	Leadership	Middle Management	Frontline
#7 How do we know it's working?	Use a monthly Scorecard/Heat Map which shows progress against the plan, and input and output measures for both the priority theme and the standard operating objectives.	Use the meeting rhythm of:	Use the meeting rhythm of:
		Daily 5 minutes stand up for issues.	Daily 5 minutes stand up for issues
		Weekly staff for checking progress and adjusting.	Use a Scorecard/ Heat map
		Use a Scorecard/ Heat map.	Implement a Behaviour check
	Implement a Behaviour check.	Implement a Behaviour check.	Be a happy, focused team.
	Establish a meeting rhythm to review progress monthly.	Be a happy, focussed team.	

Table 1

Case Study: 7 Steps in Action

A large yacht paint company with a turnover of £30m had closed all but two of its nine manufacturing plants in Europe.

The plant closures were made in the autumn, a period of low demand in this highly seasonal business.

When demand increased in the spring it became apparent that the business could not cope. It was delivering about 50% of orders on time in full, against the expectation and industry norm of 95%. Unless the situation was rectified, the business would be under serious threat!

So, we worked with the team and applied the *7 Steps.*

What are we trying to get done?
The company agreed its single main priority was to restore service levels to 95% for the next season.

What are the moving parts?
Two manufacturing plants, external packaging and label suppliers, a planning team, 12 country based sales teams, a health and safety team, a research and development team to work on product development and a marketing team to launch these new products in the next season.

What is the optimum path?
We involved the key players in mapping every process from start to finish. We determined the critical path and corresponding work. We then reverse engineered the process to set the deadlines required for success.

Who is going to do the work?
The optimum path work in *Step 3* had identified the tasks required. We arranged for a manager from each department (moving part) to be accountable for interpreting the plan for their team. Making sure that front line staff understood the plan was a company priority.

How do we engage them?
We delivered several presentations and cascaded regular communications to those involved. All were aware of the importance of getting the service levels up to 95% and of their part in the solution.

What is the plan?
We drew up a plan which detailed the critical path and deadlines for all involved. An appointed project manager drove the plan, giving regular updates to all. If there was slippage to any

deadline we knew the same day. During this process it became clear that the research and development and marketing teams were planning to launch some products whose critical path took them beyond the launch date - i.e. they were setting themselves up to fail! We reset the dates and launched successfully.

How do we know it's working?

The project manager ran weekly meetings with team members and made sure they were delivering to plan. In addition, a few key input and output measures were agreed. These were shared with the whole team, so all could see progress and issues that needed addressing.

The key output measure was, of course, the in full on time service level and this rose from 50% to 98.5% - the best in the industry. The service level was now a competitive advantage!

I get a real buzz from using the 7 Step Blueprint to help teams work together effectively, solve big problems and drive real business performance. If you'd like to discuss our approach in more detail, let's chat.

References

- Lencioni. P. (2002). *The Five Dysfunctions of a Team: A Leadership Fable.* Jossey-Bass.

- Wiseman. E. And Mckeown. G. (2010). *Multipliers: How the Best Leaders Make Everyone Smarter.* HarperCollins Publishers

Ian Thomas is highly effective Strategy and Teamwork Consultant.

He has over 35 years' experience, latterly as a senior director, gained with blue chip market leaders *BP, Castrol* and *International Paint.*

His early career began in R&D from where he moved on to successful roles in sales, marketing, commercial operations and supply chain. Consequently, he has a thorough understanding of the key business functions and how they interact in successful companies.

It was later, when he led large cross-functional and multinational transformation programmes such as, post-merger integration, global strategy implementation and supply chain restructuring that he discovered the critical importance of effective teamwork and his passion for leading and motivating teams.

He founded *IPT*, a business consultancy which focuses on helping business leaders improve the performance of their organisations.

IPT uses the *7 Step Blueprint* to challenge and help senior leaders develop clear strategies and build a winning teamwork culture to execute those strategies successfully.

hello@ianpthomas.com

www.ianpthomas.com

www.linkedin.com/in/ianpthomas/

Emerging Trends

Innovation, disruption, new thinking, gaps in the market, emerging industries, emerging trends, transitions, transformations

Social Leadership

Jill Chitty

If ever we lived in a time when there was a tremendous need for strong, purposeful leadership, full of integrity and common sense with the willingness to step up, it is now.

In a world of a million followers it's easy to slip into being comfortable, like a familiar pair of slippers and enjoy the status of tribe member, in the benefit zone as the one who receives all the value.

Leadership can seem a distant hope, a dream even. Utopia.

We all need to belong and gain insight from someone who is a few steps further along the road than us, but all too often it's the place we come to rest, and we fail to discover the leader within.

The voice within us all cries out to be heard, it was put there for a purpose...to be discovered...to be shared. Your story is unique, it's vital and it's missing if you do not step up and lead in the world.

This book is a testimony to the fact that leadership comes in many guises and is vital for a whole variety of reasons. You will have your own experiences of both good and bad leadership.

You will have been formed by your experiences and they will colour not just whether you choose to step up as a leader, but how you behave as a leader.

Leadership is required within every aspect of business, some indisputable and obvious, others less so.

The moderately new world of social media is a key area where those that lead, and lead well stand out, not simply head and shoulders above their peers, but mountains above them.

It's clear to see that many are desecrating social media through lack of understanding; believing they can translate 'old ways' of marketing and selling onto new platforms that have come to require distinct approaches of thinking and behaving.

The 'hard sell format' on all social platform breeds disgust, distrust and brings many potential relationships to an abrupt end. It sours the mouths of its recipients who in turn proclaim that social is not the way forward for business.

This breed of behaviour is a malady that is symptomatic of being stuck, generating thoughtless activity that creates nothing more than noise and a high level of pissosity.

The remedy to this of course is…

Leadership.

Leadership and LinkedIn

Working on *LinkedIn* as my platform of choice in the business to business market I see this inferior behaviour modelled all the time.

Too many people join *LinkedIn* thinking that their mere presence alone will draw perfect prospects to them…'build it and they will come'…I think not!

As a result, *LinkedIn* to them is nothing more than on online CV. They upload their details on to the platform, stating their role, business name and the features of what the business does.

It's operational and nothing more. 2D.

They begin growing their network, slowly at first, but it soon gathers pace. Before they know it, they have a thousand plus connections. It feels good and they are ambitious to grow a bigger network.

Recognising it's a numbers game they continue, more connections equals more sales, right?

Caution is thrown to the wind and connections are made at pace, but with little thought. It feels good to be sitting on such a large network, it feeds the ego.

But, as of to date there has not been a sniff of interest in their services, no monies have exchanged … strange.

They heard it was a good idea to message people on *LinkedIn,* so … they message away to their network sharing who they are and what they do.

It's a no brainer, surely?

People start responding back.

Messages are received demanding to be removed from all future messaging. Some are not so polite, whilst others respond with the standard *not for me* reply.

It leaves a sour taste in the mouth but that's business, eh?

Until, *LinkedIn* themselves send a message.

A warning.

Too many people have reported their activity as spam. Stop or you'll be thrown off!

What to do now?

The *Home Feed.*

This is it!

The chance to get their message out to millions …

Multiple times a day links placed on the home feed sending willing candidates to their website.

Every time they write a blog they post it on the home feed.

They check for clicks and comments, but it's a ghost town.

Tumbleweed.

Hours of blood, sweat and tears.

All for nothing.

It's time to *do* something different.

It's time to *be* something different.

It's time to step up and lead.

If you have read the last passage thinking 'Ugh! I've done that!' to any of those mistakes – take heart. That is the exact story of how I behaved on *LinkedIn* when I first started on the platform until I decided to step up, learn a better way and lead.

The results were not just crazily good but almost instant.

Within two weeks I won two contracts worth £21,000. But better than that was the fact that people were not just willing to listen to me and engage with me but were looking out for my content.

Let me share with you the three crucial changes I made that marked my transition from flounderer to leader.

There are just two things your market wants.

- A desire for something more
- A desire for something less

Now, this might be marketing 101 for some of you but often we're so close to what's going on in our work and businesses that we miss it. Your first step to leading well on *LinkedIn* is to let your market know that you can create within them the very transformation they want; more of something or less of something.

Knowing your market better than anyone else in the world is key.

Creating *client facing* content is the optimum way and will lead your Profile visitors along a very different path.

If my *Professional Headline* reads 'Director of ...' that is all about me, but if it says, *Making Monthly Accounts Easy for Solopreneurs* and *SME's* that all about them. *[Your Professional Headline is the 120 characters under your name :)]*

If you continue to make your *LinkedIn* marketing about you it will never be about them, your market whom you are trying to reach, and as consumers they're only interested in *WIIFT* – what's in it for them.

Lead with your knowledge of their current situation and how it feels for them to be where they are right now. Offer some easy steps they can take to begin seeing a step change. Be bold and share your back story and of how you arrived at your transformation and all the key lessons you learnt along the way.

Use every possible area of *LinkedIn* to convey hope for something better ahead and start multiple conversations with them.

Get involved. Engage with all who engage with you.

Even your *Experience Section* can be the full 2,000 characters and should speak of the experiences you have had, the lessons you have learned and thinking that has developed to take you awesome at what you do now.

KEY TIP: Take a look at your *LinkedIn Profile* and if there are more than 1-2 'we', 'I' 'me' 'my' 'our' and 'us' it's all about you and not about them.

Stay Social

Social media is called 'social' for a reason!

It's a place to interact and engage. To dissect thoughts, debate subjects and share knowledge and expertise.

People want to be part of the conversation.

Magically, if you are engaging correctly, trust and credibility is built quickly along the way. The trust and credibility that is an essential part of generating leads and more importantly, sales.

Just this year there has been a huge shift in the way people are interacting on LinkedIn. The home feed has come alive with engagement. It's not the blog posts that are getting the attention but the thought leader's posts.

Using up every last character available, members are writing long form posts of their experiences, feelings, and perceptions of their industry.

It's littered with stories and ramblings that don't just engage thousands of people but hundreds of thousands. They lead with integrity, vulnerability, honesty and truthfulness. It's often messy, bold or controversial but their audience loves it, laps it up and engages at high levels with it.

These *LinkedIn* engagers are bold, brave and willing to abandon the pride, bare all for the chance to build huge trust and love.

I've experienced huge sales from a single post that took just five minutes to write and had 27,000+ views.

This kind of success comes from a willingness to ditch the front that we all too often hide behind and share the raw, butt-naked truth of all that matters to be us in our skin and position.

It comes from a readiness to break out, do something different and lead.

KEY TIP: If your posts aren't getting any traction on the *Home* feed, you simply haven't understood you market deeply enough to engage them.

Opportunities ... maybe clients

Like most people, you must have heard of some of the incredible stories of new clients that businesses are finding on *LinkedIn?* Or are they?

My take is that there are opportunities on *LinkedIn*, not clients. There are prospects wanting something who are on *LinkedIn*, but not clients.

The secret sauce is finding those opportunities and leading them off *LinkedIn* to continue the journey with you.

I speak to hundreds of different business owners each month and it's rare to find a business with systems and processes that continually work in bringing in a steady, consistent and predictable flow of leads.

Your final stage of leadership on social media is to lead them along a clear path through a buying process, handling their objections, giving them clear steps and the opportunity to 'self-select', raise their hand and say, 'I'm in!'

It's true that a sale is rarely clinched on *LinkedIn* or any other social platform. The relationship is only discovered and begins to build.

It's at this point that you must be clear where you want to take your leads. Where is the best place for them to have their questions answered, fears allayed and objections resolved?

How can you best serve them at this crucial time for both of you and create the transformation they desire?

LinkedIn provides a ton of opportunities such as *Media, Projects* and *Links* that can offer an avenue to move away from *LinkedIn,* giving you the chance to diagnose their issue, add value and build the relationship.

You will need to choose what is right for your particular market and situation. It could be that sending them to a scheduling page to book a phone call or face to face meeting is your best option for converting leads. For others it may be a landing page that works best or a page on your website *LinkedIn* is a marketing tool, and only that. Any old fool can master its features. (I'm testimony to that!) but it takes a leader to generate a system that constantly delivers and adds value along the way.

Each step should address a specific problem or desired result, whether it's content that adds value and builds credibility, or strategy sessions that diagnose the current issues that are keeping your prospect stuck.

Once these systems are in place, it's your job to step up and lead prospects through them. People will always want to short cut access to getting your value, but these systems qualify prospects, reducing the time-wasting element of lead generation that can so often occur. They are a great way to solidify the relationship along the way.

You will now be in a position to advise which one of your products or services is best for each prospect so that you can continue to serve and lead them in the most transformational way.

KEY TIP: When building your sales funnel on *LinkedIn*, your *Profile* should be at the heart of it. Especially if you're a leader.

Step Up and Serve

When used correctly social media can be a tremendous platform to display your unique skills and offering. It creates a space to discover the gems of opportunity that are hiding with in it.

It requires that we step up, stand out and steer those who connect, follow and like into a meaningful relationship of nurture, value and exchange.

It demands our honesty, our integrity, our courage.

To lead is to transform.

To lead is to serve.

To lead is to love.

Jill Chitty is a *LinkedIn* Marketing Expert who has been helping clients generate leads through LinkedIn for over five years. She makes the complicated simple!

Jill doesn't just show you how to use the features of *LinkedIn*…Oh no! What sets her apart is her ability to transform a broken profile into a compelling marketing hub.

Using *LinkedIn* marketing strategies, she creates fills and floods the *LinkedIn* sales funnel.

Jill's journey with *LinkedIn* began after she sold her first business and it was not a pretty start!

She made every mistake known to business on *LinkedIn* and was on the verge of being thrown off *LinkedIn* when she decided it was time to learn how to use the platform properly.

She's so glad she invested that time and now generates thousands of pounds for her clients.

Jill now offers *LinkedIn* marketing training to a wide variety of industries including IT, Recruitment, Coaching, Trainers, Printers, Marketing Agencies, Estate Agents. Graphic Designers, Travel, Law, and Personal Services.

Her signature system, developed over the years, takes each student on a path of clarity to creating growth within their business.

She has two grown up boys who have suddenly realised the power of *LinkedIn* for their careers who now regularly get free training and help!

https://uk.linkedin.com/in/jillchitty

Business Leadership Profiling

Andrew Priestley

A client needed to hire top 5% talent for a technical, highly responsible, hard-to-fill leadership role in a high-risk, high-compliance industry.

As you might expect they advertised the position, fielded a host of impressive CVs, whittled the applicants down to a suitable short-list and commenced round-one interviews.

They did thorough qualification, referee and reference checks and commenced a second round of interviews.

From there they narrowed the list down even further and then asked me to profile the remaining three candidates.

Each candidate completed a questionnaire that generated a report and a series of charts.

Understand, any one of the three candidates was suitable for the role. My role was to give an indication of what sort of management, training, monitoring and supervision support the successful client might need *once hired*.

My role was *not* to recommend who to hire. No one gets hired or fired on how they complete a questionnaire.

On the following page is a small sample of a profiling tool I developed called the *Business Leadership Profile*. This is a tiny fraction of a 10-page report and I want to demonstrate the value of profiling leaders.

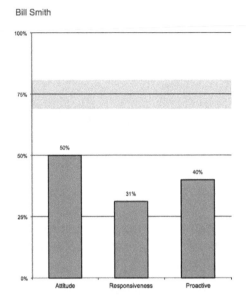

Here's how to read it.

On the left hand side is a scale 0-100%. At the 75% mark is a horizontal band that ranges between 70 and 80%.

The chart displays a total of 36 traits associated with high performance in a leadership role. In this example I've featured just three traits: *Attitude, Responsiveness* and *Proactive.*

The vertical bars need to be *inside* that horizontal bandwidth. If the bars are *outside* the horizontal bandwidth - *high or low* - it indicates coaching targets.

If you were hiring Bill here's what I could tell you:

- I know *Bill Smith* (not his real name) will interview well.
- And I know you will like him.

But I also know:

- Bill is a *glass-half-empty* guy

FIT-FOR-PURPOSE LEADERSHIP #2

- I know if you give him an idea or an opinion he'll be a *yes-but* guy. He will tell you *why it won't work*

- After a time, you will eventually find Bill *both* negative and critical.

- He will immerse in problems and often take too long to resolve issues

- I can predict he will neglect important problems

- I would expect Bill to create a *culture of blame.* And there will *always* be some reason why you can't blame Bill for lack of results. *It will never be his fault.*

That's just the first three bars.

For your reference, for optimum high performance, you need scores of around 75%. (By the way we are not looking for 100%. There are no 100% people. On this chart system scores out of range on the high side are also coaching targets).

This chart is very easy for anyone to read because for optimum performance the bars need to be *inside* the horizontal bandwidth and in this case you can *see* that they aren't.

Let's look at each trait starting with Bill's *Attitude* score.

Attitude measures how positive and optimistic you feel about life and situations. It's a general indication of resilience, too.

Bill's score is 50%.

A low score on *Attitude* suggests Bill is a *glass half empty* sort of guy. Bill will actually get paid to be *analytical* and to *critique* situations and make careful decisions based on discernment. But Bill is trending towards negative and critical.

And you've worked with people like Bill. They are hard work. They will *yes-but* any idea you put forward and eventually you stop putting forward ideas.

Look at his *Responsiveness* score.

Responsiveness measures your ability to respond to problems.

A low score of 31% usually indicates what I call a *nice guy*. *Nice guys* person initially present as friendly, agreeable, affable, easy-going ... *and nice*. This low *Responsiveness* score indicates he will interview well and you will like him.

No surprise: *nice guys* want to be liked. And I can predict Bill will prioritise being liked over being respected.

I can predict he will react to problems slowly. He will immerse in the problem, put off making key decisions and cause delays. Eventually it will show up as costly productivity and effectiveness issues.

Let's look at *Proactive*.

Proactive measures perceived *locus of control*. Basically, do you feel you are in charge of your own life or are you at the effect of what's happening?

A score of 41% suggests Bill doesn't *feel* in control - *things just happen to him*. But when there's a problem, he will push responsibility and accountability away. There will always be very *logical* reasons - usually technicalities - for why he couldn't get the result and therefore why you can't blame him.

I can predict he will direct the blame to something or someone else.

OK, it sounds like I've just thrown Bill under a bus! But I want to emphasise, left to his own devices - *under pressure* - this is Bill's default position.

They should consider Bill because he has all the qualifications and experience they need. My client knows it is very hard to find someone with Bill's skill set. So it would be silly to let someone of Bill's calibre get away.

I was giving my client feedback on how to best monitor, manage and supervise Bill in that key leadership role. The good news is: because we *can* flag potential problems ahead of time my client's *can* determine a strategy to leverage his strengths and mitigate his weaknesses.

I went through the entire *Business Leadership Profile (BLP)* in detail with my client and made the following recommendations:

- If you hire Bill, give him a *very clear job description*.

- Set very clear and specific targets and KPIs.

- Include regular formal and informal performance reviews.

- In meetings, get Bill to focus on the positive because Bill will *automatically* want to go to the negative. Ask him to explore *what's right* with an idea before he tells you *what's wrong* with an idea.

- Under the pressure of deadlines, *expect* Bill to behave like a *prima donna* and observe if he uses his *qualifications*, experience and technical knowledge as a smokescreen. Pay close attention if you feel inferior and back down.

- Pay very close attention to the morale of staff who work with Bill and monitor for frustration. Importantly, monitor for good staff who start making noises that they want to find another job!

- Closely monitor the problems that *will* gather around him in the first three months. Pay close attention to how Bill resolves issues but importantly how responsive he is. *Or isn't.*

- Pay very close attention to any excuses for delays, inaction and check the veracity of those excuses.

- Closely monitor the *cost* of delays.

- Pay attention if you start mentally managing Bill and very close attention if you find yourself doing aspects of his role for him.

- Bill **is not** a *set-and-forget* hire. If you hire Bill, offer him a strict three to six month probation period which you can enact at any time. Bill *will* dazzle you in months one to three. The key is monitoring and supervision.

So what happened?

They hired Bill with those recommendations.

As predicted, it started really well. In the first few weeks Bill definitely impressed everyone. It seemed like a perfect match. He was friendly, charming and likable and fitted in very quickly. People quickly appreciated his knowledge, experience and wisdom.

But by the fourth month, my client was showing the first signs of frustration. Bill was very knowledgeable, of course, but he introspected and vacillated on key decisions.

His staff began making noises that it was hard to get Bill to make even benign decisions.

Within five months my client found himself mentally managing routine problems and solving larger ones Bill failed to resolve. Predictably, Bill always had a good reason why delays were necessary and why he couldn't make key decisions. And, of course, how he was under-resourced or why his team were letting him down.

Within six months, team morale was at an all-time low. Key staff were seeking off-the-record meetings with the managing director. And then two valuable long-standing staff members resigned.

In month seven, Bill fumbled a major contract. And as predicted, it wasn't his fault. His team failed to give him the information he needed to make a decision. When asked why he didn't raise those issues at management meetings he said, 'I felt I was handling things' and 'I didn't want to bother the directors.'

By month eight Bill was finally asked to leave.

Bill was put on *garden leave* and immediately engaged an employment lawyer and filed for a settlement agreement. It then emerged that he had an existing settlement agreement that gagged his previous employer from saying anything prejudicial about Bill. And now he wanted the *same* settlement agreement and a pay-out to exit quietly and expediently.

My client signed the agreement and paid him out.

At this point the company called me back to debrief. *What did we miss? Could Bill have been an asset?*

The answer is Bill was great asset.

I asked if they had followed my recommendations but they admitted that the first few weeks went so well that they went hands-off. They *set-and-forgot.*

Can we know this ahead of time?

I'm going to argue that human behaviour is quite predictable. Once you get into a way of behaving - good or bad - you tend to stick closely to that way of with that behaving.

And we know a lot about effective leadership.

Two well accepted factors of leadership are *task* and *relation-ships*. *Task* is the ability to get things done - get results - and this incorporates the leader's strategic vision about what needs to be achieved and why; and *relationships* is the ability to inspire, motivate and get along with others.

The *Business Leadership Profile (BLP)* answers questions about *task* and *relationship*. In addition it incorporates aspects of the *Five Factor Model of Personality (Costa and McCrae);* and then extrapolates those five factors into 36 sub traits associated with high performance in a leadership role.

The *BLP* does not incorporate clinical filters so it will *not* tell me if you are anxious or depressed, for example. But it will tell me where you will most likely go under pressure. And from that we can *reasonably* construct a snapshot of your leadership behaviour with a degree of workable accuracy.

Overall, Bill's *BLP* indicates that while he is ambitious, he takes on far too many projects and subsequently has a trail of unfinished projects (results). Under pressure he goes hands-off and then when the project predictably drags or stalls he will then blame his team (relations). His team get to know this about Bill which creates a culture of low morale and then blame.

And that is exactly what happened.

So if all that was predictable why did they hire him?

Be clear: profiles are not intended as a hiring or firing tool. No one gets hired or fired based on how they fill in a questionnaire. Today the decision to recruit is based on a battery of assessments including the interview, reference checks and so on.

And there are no perfect people.

Because it is hard to find someone with Bill's experience and qualifications you should hire. My profile tool is designed to help my clients better-manage new and existing staff.

In Bill's case, I provided specific feedback to enable them to effectively to maximise his assets and mitigate his shortcomings. In essence, the *BLP* is designed to help my client go into that relationship with eyes wide open.

That works as long as you act on the advice!

The *BLP* is also used as a pre-coaching, benchmarking tool.

So does profiling work for leaders?

I have to say it does. But I am biased. I have successfully used profiling for over 20 years. As a leader profiling can shave years off your learning time.

And obviously, I like profiling because I helped adapt this tool for business leadership across a broad and diverse range of commercial settings.

Of course, there are other equally useful profiling tools that are commercially available. You might have used instruments like *DISC*, the *Myers-Briggs Type Indicator (MBTI)*, the *Minnesota Multiphasic Personality Inventory (MMPI)*, the *Strengths* test, the *Hogan Personality Inventory (HPI)*, the Enneagram and new comers to the industry such as *Talent Dynamics*. All of them good in their own way.

Some of these tools are high-end psychometric instruments that can *only* be administered by a registered psychologist (i.e., *MMPI*); some are pseudo-psychometric instruments that require intensive training but still only delivered by a trained and registered agent *(MBTI, DISC);* and many are *pop quizzes* capable of delivering a useful, albeit, general snapshot delivered by non-qualified professionals.

Some are incomprehensibly complex and interpreting them is both a science and an art form. A lot of instruments cannot be easily understood or interpreted by either the client or the respondent. Some lack any substance, science or utility.

My biggest criticism is many profiling tools are written by academics with little real-world commercial experience. Subsequently, many are interesting but not useful.

I qualified in organisational and industrial psychology *and* I've run companies so I wanted a tool that made commercial sense. I wanted a report I could understand at a glance.

And because I specialise in practical leadership I wanted a tool that could pinpoint specific coaching and mentoring targets and not overwhelm me or my client with too many things to address. (As an example I recently viewed a profiling tool that identified 84 coaching targets! Where would you even start?)

By contrast Bill's chart identifies five clear coaching targets.

For starters Bill's leadership will improve if he consciously works on his *attitude*. Bill gets paid to be analytical but over time I suspect that has skewed towards being negative and critical. He needs to force himself to focus on the positives.

I would coach him on the difference between *critiquing* and being critical.

Bill needs to become more *responsive* to problems. He needs to resolve problems more efficiently and effectively.

I would get Bill to *collect problems* impacting his role; and monitor how he was *handling* those problems. The famous 1980s *GROW* model *(Goal, Reality, Options, Will or Wrap-Up)* is *still* an elegantly simple but highly effective coaching tool that facilitates reflection that drives accountability and action.

I would get Bill to *collect excuses* for delays and inaction.

And I would certainly increase his awareness on the difference between *busy* or *productive.*

That would help Bill to feel more in control and would help him to become more proactive.

Importantly, improving those three traits would improve his relationships and his team culture.

The chemistry between a coach and client, a robust framework for business leadership and a non-invasive, reflective coaching or mentoring framework works incredibly well, but only if it's first based on high-grade information about how you perform as a leader.

In my experience, profiling tools provide that clarity.

Is it clear?

I would stress again that the feedback is clear, easy to understand, in plain language, genuinely relevant and useful to the respondent. A lot of tools I've seen are neither relevant, easy to understand, meaningful or useful.

Often feedback is skewed in favour of the theory underpinning the tool. In essence, the respondent and their situation is shoe horned into the theory. I recently chatted with a new client who was told he was anxious and depressed and lacked emotional intelligence. When we chatted it became clear that he was trying to run a sophisticated manufacturing division with 30 year old software! He did not have a clinical issue - he was frustrated. (By the way, the person who delivered that diagnosis was not qualified to provide a clinical opinion.)

I am always interested in what respondents do with their profiles *after* profiling. In a lot of cases profiling is a tick-the-box exercise that goes no further.

I have seen companies pour thousands into leadership development assessments that were interesting but ultimately had zero impact.

Profiling should leave an organisation better off in both the short and long term, and certainly not create a cultural risk that leaves the company worse off.

Whatever tool you select, profiling is invaluable if it benefits the respondent and the company.

Profiling should ultimately offer a positive, professional, affirming experience and change people and situations for the better.

But for leaders I believe profiling more than justifies any expense if it leads to positive changes in behaviour that balances the need to achieve results and build solid relationships.

References

- Carver & Scheier. (2004). *Perspectives on Personality.*

- Costa, P.T. & McCrae, R. (1992). *NEO Personality Inventory: NEO PI and NEO Five Factor Inventory* (Professional Manual) Odessa.

- Nettle, D. (2007). *Personality: What makes you the way you are.* Oxford University Press

Andrew R Priestley is an award winning business leadership coach, qualified in industrial and organisational psychology.

He has written three #1 ranked business books, is an in-demand speaker and trainer and was listed in the *2017 UK Top 100 Entrepreneur Mentors.*

The *Business Leadership Profile (BLP)* is used by companies worldwide and is available globally in English, French and Spanish. It is used as a stand alone instrument or used as a prescreening precoaching benchmark used in conjunction with his business leadership development programmes delivered worldwide.

If you are interested in the *BLP* or becoming a *BLP* coach please contact Andrew via the *Contact* links at:

www.andrewpriestley.com

Join Leadership Gigs

Would you like to be a part of *Leadership Gigs*? *Leadership Gigs* is a conversation for leaders worldwide. Here's how it works.

Think of it like a private members club – you can dip in and dip out as you wish – there is no pressure to show up.

Currently it is free to join. A good way to get involved is by starting with the *Facebook* group:

http://bit.ly/LeadershipGigsFB

Leadership Gigs is a support network so if you need high-end help/support then ask the group (you'll be nicely surprised). Our aim for this is to build a thriving community of leaders who are helping each other's journey into the next decade.

Lastly, thank you for purchasing *Fit-For-Purpose Leadership #2.* I would love your feedback.

Watch out for *Fit-For-Purpose Leadership #3*, coming soon!

Did you miss Fit-For-Purpose Leadership #1?

Relax! It's our best-selling Fit-For-Purpose #1
is available on *Amazon* as both paperback and *Kindle*.
18 inspired business leaders give their highest-value,
current best thinking on leadership.

Lightning Source UK Ltd.
Milton Keynes UK
UKHW02f1000131217
314388UK00006B/109/P